A Practical Guide to

EFFECTIVE
SCHOOL BOARD
MEETINGS

A Practical Guide to

EFFECTIVE SCHOOL BOARD MEETINGS

Rene S. Townsend • James R. Brown • Walter L. Buster

CORWIN PRESS
A SAGE Publications Company
Thousand Oaks, California

For information:

Corwin Press
A Sage Publications Company
2455 Teller Road
Thousand Oaks, California 91320
www.corwinpress.com

Sage Publications Ltd.
1 Oliver's Yard
55 City Road
London EC1Y 1SP
United Kingdom

Sage Publications India Pvt. Ltd.
B-42, Panchsheel Enclave
Post Box 4109
New Delhi 110 017 India

Printed in the United States of America.

Library of Congress Cataloging-in-Publication Data

Townsend, Rene S.
   A practical guide to effective school board meetings / Rene S. Townsend,
James R. Brown, Walter L. Buster.
      p. cm.
Includes bibliographical references and index.
ISBN 1-4129-1328-4 (cloth) — ISBN 1-4129-1329-2 (pbk.)
   1. School boards—United States. 2. Public meetings—United States. 3. School board members—United States. I. Brown, James R. (James Russell), 1942- II. Buster, Walter L. III. Title
LB2831.T65 2005
379.1′531—dc22   2004025336

This book is printed on acid-free paper.

05   06   07   08   09   10   9   8   7   6   5   4   3   2   1

Acquisitions Editor:	Elizabeth Brenkus
Editorial Assistant:	Candice L. Ling
Production Editor:	Laureen A. Shea
Copy Editor:	Teresa R. Herlinger
Typesetter:	C&M Digitals (P) Ltd.
Proofreader:	Sue Irwin
Indexer:	Michael Ferreira
Cover Designer:	Anthony Paular

Contents

Foreword

This book provides specific, practical, feasible, and effective advice for how boards and administrators can perform their multiple roles well. The authors focus the board on the right issues and duties with a major emphasis on teaching and learning. They start with the "right mission" for the board and then demonstrate in detail how to translate this into building a superintendent leadership team. The major focus is on helping superintendents to prepare, conduct, and implement board meetings that flow from the board's mission and interactions with administrators. The authors provide a detailed road map for all these meeting concepts and procedures.

This book is timely and necessary because in the past two decades, criticism of school boards has intensified. Frequent allegations about inadequate pupil attainment and the collapse of big-city schools have been major media stories. Some big-city mayors have taken over the schools and eliminated the school board. One influential commentator, Chester Finn, President of the Fordham Foundation, labeled boards a "dinosaur left over from the agrarian past" and part of a wasteful middle management system. Frequently, school reforms have focused on the school site and have not addressed the board. NCLB has created a whole new direct policy and oversight system connecting federal and state governments to school site performance, bypassing the central school board.

Part of the challenge for school boards is all the things they must do according to state law and local tradition. Boards must create long-range policies, solve short-term crises, juggle federal and state mandates, discipline students, and oversee expenditures. All of these functions are impacted by shifting coalitions of teachers, community residents, students, state officials, and all kinds of reformers.

The last major change in the structure and roles of urban school boards took place between 1900 and 1920. By 1910, the conventional wisdom had evolved among school people and the leading business and professional men who spearheaded the reforms. The governance structure needed to be revised so that school boards would be small, elected at large, and purged of all connections with political parties and officials of general government, such as mayors and councilmen.

While the turn-of-the-century reformers tried to model the revamped school board on the big corporations, they left the board with a mandate to oversee and become involved in all areas of local school operation. The American school board combines the legislative, executive, and judicial functions of government. This role is too expansive and often leads boards to try to do everything by not doing much of anything in depth. This book helps superintendents establish board meetings that deal effectively with challenging multiple board roles.

School boards play a *legislative* role when they adopt budgets, pass regulations, and set policies. Moreover, they provide the constituent-services component of a legislator's district office. Parents will phone board members about fixing showers in locker rooms, relocating school crossing guards, and reclassifying children placed in special education. Many board members believe that an essential part of their role is to "fix" these individual complaints, because failure to respond may mean defeat at the polls.

School boards play an *executive* role when they implement policy. Many school boards approve not only the budget, but also almost every expenditure and contract for services. For example, a half-day consulting fee for a university professor must be approved by the school board. The board performs the same role as the U.S. Department of Education's contracting office and the General Accounting Office. Many boards approve the appointments of principals, vice principals, categorical program administrators, and even teachers.

Judicial hearings concerning students' suspensions, expulsions, inter-district transfers, and pupil placements can consume an enormous amount of time. After all administrative remedies are exhausted, the board is the final body for appeal, though citizens may still turn to the courts in some cases. Can any school board composed primarily of part-time lay people perform all these functions well? Often, board meetings are dominated by administration progress reports and parental complaints about very specific needs. Moreover, state "sunshine laws" require boards to conduct all business, including many personnel matters, in the public sessions. Does the essential policymaking role of the board suffer as other roles and functions become more important?

Superintendents and school boards who utilize this book will come a long way toward fulfilling their complex and multiple goals. They will have a much better way to interact with the many actors who come to the board for help with concerns and problems. If many boards use this book as a guide, some of their critics will have much less to say.

Michael W. Kirst
Professor of Education, Stanford University

Preface

*Here is Edward Bear, coming downstairs now, bump, bump, bump, on
the back of his head, behind Christopher Robin. It is, as far as he knows,
the only way of coming downstairs, but sometimes he feels that there
really is another way, if only he could stop bumping for a moment and
think of it.*

(A.A. Milne, 1926, p. 3)

Why would anyone write, or read, a book on board meetings? The
answer is simple: Board meetings have the potential to impact, in
a very direct way, the quality of teaching and learning in a school district.

A good board meeting contributes to the achievement of district goals. It
opens the door to student success. A poor meeting may have the opposite
effect even to the point of creating confusion and dissension throughout the
district. That is why we think it is important for every superintendent to
stop and think about his or her board meetings and consider ways to make
them more effective. When superintendents are clear about the strategies
and actions that lead to effective board meetings, they are better equipped
to help their board members meet their responsibilities to ensure high-
quality teaching and learning.

Board meetings are mission-critical work for superintendents and
board members for several reasons. The first reason is simple—the right
actions of the board result in policies and decisions directly affecting
student achievement. A board thoughtfully deliberating a proposed
policy that will lead to more students being able to enroll in Advanced
Placement classes is doing its job better than a board debating the most
recent phone bill.

Second, the time and commitment put into these activities of preparing for, conducting, following up after, and recovering from board meetings is considerable. So, if we are doing all this work, it only makes sense
for us to do the right work so the board meeting truly makes a difference
in the quality of teaching and learning.

This leads to the third reason with which all superintendents are familiar, namely the impact of board meetings on those who work directly with the board along with many others throughout the district. What people hear and see, and how they are treated, sends a strong message about "how we do things around here" and what the values are. That, of course, carries over to the students we serve.

A fourth reason is that board meetings are a focal point in forming public opinions about the quality of education in the individual district and of public education in general. In most locations, press coverage of board meetings is extensive, and many districts televise their meetings. As a result, board meetings play a significant role in increasing or decreasing public confidence in the local educational system.

Finally, we believe board meetings strongly influence board and superintendent relations, for good or ill, and that the meetings reflect and define the nature of these relations. Good board meetings strengthen superintendent–board relations; poor ones weaken those relations.

These reasons are the basis for our belief that superintendents and board members ought to give more attention to ensuring that board meetings contribute to student achievement and model the principles of good teaching and learning. Unfortunately, this is not always the case. We often hear conversations from our colleagues that indicate concern about the quality of board meetings and their impact on the important work of the district. For some superintendents, board meetings become something to get through, to check off the to-do list, and to sigh with relief when they are over so they can get on to their real work. Or worse—in some districts the meetings become entertainment and create a negative impression about the quality of education.

Superintendents often describe the anxiety they feel about upcoming board meetings; they always worry about what might go wrong. There is no denying the potential of something unusual happening on any night, at any meeting. Yet, we believe—because we have seen many powerful examples—that board meetings offer the best opportunity for moving districts forward to achieve their stated goals. Each part of this book relates to creating these meetings, starting with the big picture—the mental model of board meetings themselves.

Part I focuses on teaching and learning, for that is the heart of the matter. Board members are civic leaders; so are superintendents. Together they form the governance team with significant power and responsibilities that impact the students, staff, and other district stakeholders. Being an effective leader requires the superintendent to attend to detail on many levels and in various situations. Despite the complexity and competing demands, the governance team must focus the district's attention on the importance of powerful teaching and learning that will lead to student achievement. The outcome of the board's actions must result in supporting what goes on in the classrooms so all students can learn and achieve their goals.

Part I continues with thoughts about building the superintendent–board team. Board members and superintendents have some responsibilities in common, but there are many that are distinct and unique to their position. Role confusion leads to wasted time, lowered morale, interpersonal difficulties, and resentment. When each person fills the proper role and carries out the proper responsibilities, the likelihood of achieving district goals increases.

Knowing one's "job" is the first step, but is not enough. Boards and superintendents need to spend time reaching agreement on how they will operate with each other as they lead the district. What are the general operating procedures, the protocols, by which they will govern the district? The board and superintendent must be clear with each other and agree on how they will govern. The staff and community also need to be clear as to the roles of the superintendent and board members; they need to know what they can expect and what the limitations are for their district's leaders.

Our experience is that few governance teams have discussed role differentiation, nor have they developed operating procedures. We offer suggestions to assist superintendents and board members in this effort. Operating procedures are a precursor and foundation for planning and carrying out effective board meetings.

A board meeting is not just a task to check off the "to do" list; it is an important path to reaching the district's goals. Board meetings also are the litmus test of board and superintendent relations. Good board and superintendent relations translate into effective work on behalf of students. That is why we say board meetings are mission critical.

Productive board meetings do not just happen. Careful planning is essential, and the quality of that planning impacts directly the effectiveness of a meeting. Part II focuses on preparing the agenda and preparing for the meeting itself. Superintendents must know how to plan an agenda, organize pre-meeting details, design the board packet, and communicate the agenda to board members and other key people.

Then there is the board meeting itself—sometimes referred to as "the big show." Part III describes critical aspects of the meeting itself, from before the opening gavel to adjournment. Our philosophy is that board meetings present an opportunity to develop, emphasize, reinforce, and implement the district's mission, goals, and core values.

This philosophy is reflected in each option and suggestion we offer regarding details of the meeting. If board meetings reflect the highest priority work of the district—teaching and learning—they are far more likely to contribute directly to growth and progress of students. Ineffective, sometimes even dysfunctional, meetings detract from accomplishing the fundamental purpose—addressing student achievement. Poor meetings distract the adults, wasting precious time that should be spent in productive, proactive ways on issues related to students.

A separate chapter addresses the closed session where the board and superintendent meet in private, out of the public view. Along with basic, general guidelines reviewed by a legal firm specializing in schools, we provide some common sense tips about dealing with difficult situations.

The final section, Part IV, covers a frequently overlooked area, which is what happens after the board meeting is over. Post-meeting, the superintendent is responsible for doing or delegating many follow-up activities. Most are formal actions the staff must do, but there are also informal activities that affect and influence the culture of the district.

Then we turn our focus to the superintendent as a person. What do superintendents do for themselves, for their recovery and renewal after meetings? The connotation here is not meant to be negative; it simply acknowledges that the work of the superintendent and board members *is* frequently stressful. Therefore, it is not only useful, but also essential for you to pay attention to your recovery—your renewal.

Decisions the board is making are important, whether on routine or controversial items. Ideally, the superintendent and staff have worked hard and thoughtfully to bring forward those items for board action that they believe will improve student performance and achieve district goals. And, ideally, trustees have studied, read, considered, and made initial decisions regarding the agenda items.

All of this hard work comes together at the board meeting. After the meeting, superintendents and trustees need time for their own reflection and renewal so they can continue pursuing the district's mission and goals with passion. From experience, we know too many superintendents make the mistake of not paying attention to their own well-being, especially following the stress of preparing for and implementing board meetings.

Since the superintendent is responsible for planning board meetings and preparing the board agenda, this book addresses the superintendent. However, the book is also intended for board members, the aspiring superintendent, leadership staff, and community members. Improving school districts is a team effort. Effective board meetings are critical to this improvement effort and require the involvement and commitment of the governance team and many others in the district.

In fact, we encourage superintendents to use the book with their board members as a professional development and continuous learning tool. We see superintendents as professional educators, as coaches for school trustees. Each chapter provides opportunity for dialogue and for reaching agreements on how superintendents and trustees can improve their individual and collective effectiveness.

In each chapter, we give our opinions and advice based on years of involvement in board meetings. Among us, we have been directly responsible for well over 1,000 board meetings and have observed and studied hundreds more. We have also assisted superintendents and superintendent–board teams to increase their effectiveness.

From outstanding and effective meetings to ones that still make us shake our heads, we have seen them all. We have seen board meetings lead to positive transformations for schools, and we have seen superintendents dismissed when meetings have spun out of control.

Our goal is for you to know, and to remind you of, what a good meeting looks like, to have the benefit of understanding the specific practices that offer the best opportunity for success. We know it is possible to have effective meetings, ones connected to teaching and learning in a way that moves districts to accomplish their goals.

We believe in the old saw that "if your only tool is a hammer, the whole world is a nail." There are many tools in the superintendent's toolkit. Just as teachers continue to add to their repertoire of teaching strategies, so must the top district leadership build its capacity for continuous improvement. This requires learning about each tool, and taking time to decide, consciously, which tool to use and when to use it, and then to reflect on the outcome.

We hope you, as a superintendent, will look carefully at the options in each section, analyze your practice, and consciously decide how you can operate in the most effective way. Then we hope you will involve your board in a dialogue leading to decisions your governance team can make to improve your meetings. We offer options, but you must decide what is best for you.

Board meetings have a powerful influence on everything from district goals to district culture. For this reason it is essential that the superintendent and board members work together as a governance team to make board meetings as productive and effective as possible. It is the responsibility of the superintendent and the board leadership team to create the environment to support and sustain powerful teaching and learning that leads to student achievement.

Acknowledgments

Throughout the years, we have been blessed by our associations with outstanding educators in each of the districts where we have worked. We have also learned from our colleagues in California and around the country. They have shared their successes, their ideas, and a few experiences that usually started with, "Don't ever do this!" We thank them all for the lessons they taught us and whatever wisdom we were able to acquire.

In addition, there are some specific people we would like to acknowledge. First we thank Sharalee Jorgensen for her thoughtful and incisive comments on our rough drafts, as well as being there to help put all the details in place. Another thank you goes to Michael Smith of the law firm Lazano and Smith, specializing in schools. He kindly reviewed the chapter on closed sessions to offer suggestions and make sure our general advice was sound. We also appreciate Mike Kirst taking the time to write the foreword. His work over the years on education policy and governance has helped superintendents everywhere become better at what we do.

A number of people have done excellent work on board–superintendent relations. These include Richard Goodman, Luann Fulbright, and Bill Zimmerman, who helped us think more clearly about the responsibilities of boards and superintendents to improve student achievement. We also appreciate the ongoing fine work of the American Association of School Administrators, the National School Boards Association, the California School Boards Association, and the Association of California School Administrators, the latter two associations in the state where the three of us were superintendents.

Over our collective 52 years as superintendents and 1,000-plus school board meetings, we have worked with many school board members. We learned from them all. We send a particular note of thanks to those who serve on school boards for no other reason than to make education better for every student.

And finally, although it may seem corny, we acknowledge each other and thank each other for being friends and mentors for so many years. The book came about because we have done workshops on school board meetings for new superintendents for many years. After each workshop, participants asked us for more, which motivated us to put it in writing so practicing, new, and future superintendents will have something concrete to turn to for suggestions.

Our deep desire is that superintendents and school board members will see school board meetings as mission-critical work, and will strive together to connect everyone to teaching and learning for the achievement of all students.

The authors also thank the wonderful people at Corwin who are true professionals. We deeply appreciate the wisdom and encouragement of Elizabeth Brenkus, Acquisitions Editor; the prompt and warm responsiveness of Candice L. Ling, Editorial Assistant, and Laureen Shea, Production Editor; and the sharp eye, pen, and insights of Teresa Herlinger, Copy Editor.

The authors and Corwin Press gratefully acknowledge the contributions of the following individuals:

Betty Bennett
Assistant Professor
College of Education
University of North Florida
Jacksonville, FL

Randel Beaver
Superintendent
Archer City Independent School
   District
Archer City, TX

Chris Christensen
Superintendent
Deubrook Area School
White, SD

Janet Chrispeels
Professor
Gevirtz Graduate School
   of Education
University of California
Santa Barbara, CA

James Halley
Superintendent
North Kingstown School
   Department
North Kingstown, RI

Douglas Hesbol
Superintendent, Principal
Thomasboro Grade
   School District #130
Thomasboro, IL

Rob Kesselring
Trainer, Consultant, Author
Apple Valley, MN

Kaetlyn Lad
Director, Associate Professor
Educational Leadership
   Program
Saint Mary's College
   of California
Moraga, CA

Dan Lawson
Superintendent
Tullahoma City School
Tullahoma, TN

Jim Ritchie
Professor
Department of Educational
   Administration
San Jose State University
San Jose, CA

Glenn Sewell
Superintendent, Principal
Wheatland Union High School
    District
Wheatland, CA

Albert Thomas
Assistant Professor
Department of Educational
    Leadership
University of South Alabama
Mobile, AL

Karen Tichy
Associate Superintendent for
    Instruction
Catholic Education Office
Archdiocese of St. Louis
St. Louis, MO

Linda Vogel
Assistant Professor
College of Education
University of Northern Colorado
Greeley, CO

About the Authors

All three authors, former superintendents who served in both small and large public school districts in California, have at different times received the Robert F. Alioto Award for Instructional Leadership. In addition to their current activities, they are partners in Leadership Associates, a superintendent search firm. Also, through the consulting firm Innovative Strategies, Rene, Jim, and Walt conduct workshops for new, aspiring, and experienced superintendents, and board–superintendent teams. Jim and Rene are partners and Walt is a consultant in Innovative Strategies. Rene and Jim have each served as chair of the California State Superintendents Committee and the State Superintendents Annual Symposium. Together and separately, the three have authored many journal and newspaper articles. All three share a love of reading, running, travel, family, and service to community.

 **Rene Townsend**, former superintendent for 10 years, is Executive Director of the Urban Education Dialog (UED) and Public School Services (PSS), nonprofit organizations founded by Price Charities. The UED is a forum to confront challenges facing urban school districts and exchange best practices; PSS has a mission of reducing the price of goods and services to all public school districts. With seven other superintendents, Rene coauthored *Eight at the Top;* they are working on book two, offering more leadership insights for superintendents. Rene received her Bachelor of Science from the University of Washington, her masters from San Diego State University, and her doctorate from Northern Arizona University. She serves on the national boards of Advancement Via Individual Determination (AVID) and Educators for Social Responsibility (ESR). Her husband, Stephen Levy, is a high school principal.

James R. Brown was a superintendent for 26 years, preceded by various administrative positions and his first love, teaching history. While serving as superintendent, he chaired two major task forces, the California State Mathematics and the California High School Exit Exam. Jim is Deputy Executive Director of the Bay Area School Reform Collaborative (BASRC), and he serves on three community and education boards. Jim received his bachelor's degree from Georgetown University, his masters from the University of Kansas, and did graduate work in education administration at the University of Riverside. He is the recipient of a number of awards, including California State Superintendent of the Year in 1999 and the Marcus Foster Award in 2004. He has also served as president of the Suburban School Superintendents national group. Jim and his wife, Kathe, a librarian, have three grown sons.

Walter L. Buster is Professor of Leadership at Fresno State University and a creator of the Central Valley Educational Leadership Forum. In addition to his service as a superintendent for 19 years in three California districts, Walt was a teacher at the elementary and secondary levels, assistant principal, principal, and assistant superintendent. Recently, Walt stepped forward to serve as interim superintendent of the Fresno Unified School District, calming the district in a time of political and financial turmoil. Walt's other leadership activities include leading the Executive Leadership Academy and the Association of California School Administrators Academy. He serves on the national education advisory boards for IBM and Microsoft, and is on the board of WestEd. His bachelor's degree is from Westmont College, his masters from Chapman College, and his doctorate from the University of Montana. Walt and his wife, Susan, an artist, have two children and one grandchild.

Most spouses and families are thanked last. We would like to thank them first, for their support, love, humor, friendship, and patience—endless patience. Stephen, Kathe, and Susan are the best!

We also dedicate this work to all our colleague superintendents present, past, and future, who never lose sight of the connection of their work and that of the board to powerful teaching and learning.

A final dedication goes to Sharalee Jorgensen, whose assistance from beginning to end of this project deserves not only acknowledgment, but our deep appreciation and thanks.

PART I

The Leadership Challenge

Completing the list of tasks and activities leading to an effective school board meeting is important. However, without an understanding of and connection to the big picture of the mission and goals of a school district, the tasks end up being just that—a list. These first two chapters lay the foundation for and frame our ideas about the district's mission-critical work, so each task in the process of thinking about, preparing for, and conducting the meeting helps the board stay focused on teaching and learning.

You will read this phrase "teaching and learning" repeatedly. The reason is pretty simple—everything we do in a school district should have teaching and learning as the focus, including school board meetings.

Chapter 1 begins with understanding mission and vision, and the difference between the two, and notes the importance of staying focused on the right mission. Superintendents and boards who are clear about their mission can easily identify mission-critical work—that is, what work is the most likely to improve the quality of teaching and learning—and that leads to gains in student achievement.

Chapter 2 emphasizes how vital strong superintendent–board relationships are to creating a strong, effective, forward-moving school district. The roles of each are both distinct and complementary. Nowhere is this relationship more on display than at a board meeting. The board's primary role is policymaking and it is the superintendent's responsibility to ensure that the contents of the agenda support that role. As a framework, we share ideas based on a governance study that help the board and superintendent focus on what matters: mission, vision, structure, accountability, advocacy, and unity.

1

Focusing on Teaching and Learning

Teaching is at the heart of leading. In fact, it is through teaching that leaders lead others. . . . teaching is how ideas and values get transmitted. Therefore, in order to be a leader at all levels of an organization, a person must be a teacher. Simply put, if you aren't teaching, you aren't leading.

(Tichy, 1997, p. 71)

School districts have a single focus: teaching and learning. District goals, strategies, policies, and major activities must encourage, promote, and support excellence in teaching and learning throughout the district and in every school, every classroom, and while not often thought of, in every school board meeting. Absent this relentless focus, the message is that the district is not really serious about powerful teaching and learning. The energies and talents of staff are wasted, and student learning suffers.

The premise of this book is that the meeting of the school board is one of several mission-critical activities that occur in a school district. We believe an effective board meeting directly contributes to the achievement of the district's teaching and learning mission. An ineffective board meeting may take the district in a wrong direction and cause people inside and outside the organization to question the match between the board's actions and its statements. Inconsistency or insincerity on the part of those in leadership positions contributes to the public perception that leaders make excuses for their lack of commitment to achievement of the critical mission.

The concept of mission deserves further amplification. We will do so by examining "mission" and "mission-critical work," using examples to highlight the leadership challenge facing superintendents and school boards as they work to improve student achievement by creating the conditions that support powerful teaching and learning.

In the movie *Twelve O'Clock High*, two Central Command leaders, one a general and the other a commander, discuss possible reasons for the high casualty rates and bombing-mission failures being experienced by one of the bomber squadrons. "It's all about mission," one of them remarks. He goes on to point out how critical decisions by the base commander no longer seem to reflect fidelity to mission. In a setting familiar to other organizations, especially those highly sensitive to human relations, he states his belief that the base commander's decisions were founded on something other than the mission—in this case, the emotional well-being of one of his men. The base commander was losing sight of the squadron's mission—to destroy enemy targets (King, 1949).

The particular circumstances involved a young navigator who miscalculated the timing of a turn on the way to the target. The bombers arrived late and encountered enemy fighters. Several planes were shot down, resulting in many deaths. The base commander, however, refused to remove the navigator whose error had contributed to the mission's failure and ultimately an unnecessary loss of life. The general realized the commander was more concerned about the psyche of the navigator than about the achievement of the mission and immediately removed the base commander from his assignment.

Okay, we readily agree that school districts are not bomber squadrons even on those days when objects seem to drop down on us from nowhere. So what is the connection to teaching and learning and board meetings? We believe that school district leaders share something in common with the leaders at Central Command: mission.

Like bomber squadrons, hospitals, businesses, cities, and other organizations, school districts have a mission. We think a district's mission in its simplest form is teaching and learning. More specifically, it is to create the learning experiences that enable all students to meet high standards. Said another way, it is to give as many students as possible as many choices as possible about their lives and careers when they graduate from high school. It is our job as education leaders to make that happen.

In our research for this book, we have observed a school board that spent time at numerous meetings squabbling with each other, looking for villains to blame for low student achievement and budget problems, and allowing public board meetings to disintegrate into forums for angry citizens to attack the district and public education in general. The district had lost its focus on mission-critical work: teaching and learning. An examination of their agendas for the past year revealed that the board spent the majority of its time on political and personal agendas, scattered reports from ad hoc groups, and business issues. There was little discussion about student achievement, curriculum, or student or staff learning. Although the district's mission is posted in several places in the boardroom, the alignment of its work to this mission is absent. The words ring hollow to those attending the meeting and to staff throughout the district.

On the other hand, we have observed board meetings in districts both very large and small, where the vision, mission, and goals of the district were squarely about teaching and learning, and students were the focus of every discussion and action. Focused meetings did not mean easier meetings, for the superintendent, board, and staff took on issues that mattered, and many of them were extremely difficult. However, observers left the meetings exhilarated and hopeful because they saw people who were serious about their work and who cared about their students—*all* of their students—as well as the staff and the broader community.

MISSION IS DIFFERENT FROM VISION

Mission is not the same as vision. It is much more specific. In a sense, mission states what we do as an organization to make our vision become a reality. For example, if our vision is that of a district in which all students, except for those with the most severe disabilities, meet rigorous expectations for learning in order to become productive citizens, our mission might be to create learning paths and experiences to make that possible.

Mission defines the work we do to achieve the vision. It focuses on what we do to bring about an end result. Although we often see it cast as such, producing "productive citizens" is not a mission. The mission is what we actually do to help our students *become* productive citizens. Since it is the responsibility of everyone in the school district to contribute to the achievement of the mission, boards and superintendents must be sure that they attend to what is important and that what they do is focused on this mission. In other words, mission applies to board meetings as much as it does to classrooms and schools.

As Peter Drucker (1992) states in *Managing the Non-Profit Organization,* "What matters is the leader's mission. Therefore, the first job of the leader is to think through and define the mission of the institution" (p. 3). His words are applied directly to boards in the excellent study, *The Dynamic Board: Lessons from High-Performing Nonprofits.* The study notes, "Effective boards build their common understanding of mission and vision into most discussions." (Cvsa, Jansen, & Kilpatrick, 2003, p. 7). If vision sets direction, mission drives it. Mission focuses the district. It defines the work each person is expected to do that is mission-critical. If that work is not done well, the person should change or leave. That is true for teachers and staff, and it is true for boards and superintendents.

Given our teaching and learning mission, everything we do in a school district, including the board meeting itself, must flow from that mission. Drucker and the study mentioned above on high-performing nonprofit boards by McKinsey and Company offer some instructive thoughts on how our board agendas might become more mission focused. Drucker (1992) believes leadership must stay focused on the mission, rethink the mission as time and circumstances change, and secure resources to help the organization achieve its mission.

McKinsey (as quoted in Cvsa et al., 2003) concludes that "dynamic boards" shape direction through mission, strategy, and key policies. They make sure the organization has the resources necessary to achieve the mission and vision. They regularly reaffirm the mission, ensure decisions are consistent with the mission, hold annual workshops to reaffirm/modify the mission, and select a CEO that will move the district in the right direction. These perspectives should be at the forefront of all agenda planning.

THE RIGHT MISSION

School districts that lose focus on their mission often flounder. They undertake multiple projects and responsibilities; they take on the latest reform without ever seeking evidence as to whether that change will contribute to better teaching and learning; and they do not take on the tough accountability jobs that sometimes require a confrontation with forces that promote self interest to the detriment of student success. One indicator that the board is off course and not doing mission-critical work is when adults are fussing with adults on adult issues, rather than focusing on student learning and achievement.

Having a mission statement is not enough. Many organizations are pretty good at identifying a mission. In fact, it is hard to find a school district or school without some sort of mission statement on the wall or its Web site. The problem is that too often mission statements were developed by committees, where frustrated people finally threw in the towel and included phrases and clauses to satisfy everyone on the committee. This becomes painfully clear when people ask themselves after reading an elongated mission statement, "Now what is it exactly I'm supposed to do?" Of course, the answer is not simple or clear. Drucker (1992) confirms this when he says a mission statement should not be a "hero sandwich of good intentions . . . but a simple and clear statement" of what the organization is supposed to do (p. 5).

But it is not enough for a mission statement to have a clear focus and provide direction that mobilizes the organization around a common sense of purpose. It must also be the "right" mission. What good is a mission if it takes people in a direction they ought not go?

An excellent example of this is Captain Ahab in *Moby Dick*, who exhibits so many aspects of good leadership—vision, motivation, personal example, team building—and takes all but one of his crew to their death because the fundamental mission was flawed in the first place. Captain Ahab was blinded by his total focus on getting Moby Dick. Or there is the British colonel in *Bridge on the River Kwai* whose mission becomes the construction of the perfect bridge, rather than winning the war. His efforts to build that bridge, an act that protects his troops from their captors, but gives access to the enemy, thereby potentially costs thousands of British troops their lives while it needlessly prolongs the war (Spiegel, 1983).

When leaders are focused on the right mission, they create an energy and enthusiasm throughout the organization that motivates and inspires people. When the mission is clearly stated, people are able to decide which of all the things they do are the ones that should receive the most attention. The right mission statement, one that is clear and focused, guides the setting of goals and the establishment of priorities.

MISSION-CRITICAL WORK

However, focusing on the right mission and making it clear is not enough. It is also important to identify which work done throughout the organization is most likely to support accomplishment of the mission. We describe such work as "mission-critical"—a term with which we first became familiar when a business acquaintance in a new company described something he was doing as "mission-critical." When asked what that meant, he said very simply and clearly, "If I don't do this work well, I won't be working here." We got the point.

A few years ago, a study of the crash of ValuJet 594 (Langewiesche, 1998), in Florida demonstrated how important it is for every person in an organization to understand which pieces of work they do are mission critical. Safety was clearly a primary mission for the airline. But, somewhere in the process of loading equipment known to be unsafe (oxygen generators) on the plane, any number of people did not perform their tasks well. Some people assumed others would take care of any potential problems. All along the way, people chose not to assume personal responsibility for their actions. Others did not see their work as significant and critical to the successful flight of this ValuJet. What could loading equipment on a conveyor belt possibly have to do with safety?

These actions, along with a series of other mistakes, contributed to the tragic loss of 186 lives. Had each person in the process realized that what he or she was doing, no matter how seemingly trivial, contributed directly to the accomplishment of the company's safety mission, the tragedy would have been averted.

In school districts, as in any other organization, every person does mission-critical work. After reading the ValuJet study, a staff member in the payroll department in one district said to everyone in a district team-building workshop, that she realized for the first time how her work contributed to achievement of the district's teaching and learning mission. As she put it, "If I don't do my job well, people's paychecks could be shorted." "That," she said, "does not produce happy people, and unhappy people shouldn't be working with our children."

For teachers, an example of mission-critical work is the preparation of a lesson designed to engage all students in a learning activity to help them meet a particular standard. For a principal, it might be an agenda for a staff meeting—an agenda that includes an opportunity for professional growth. The agenda and meeting should model the kind of teaching and learning the principal wants to see in every classroom. For a playground aide, it is providing a safe and fun environment so anger and hostility do not enter the classroom after the recess. Playing background classical music in a classroom only goes so far in cooling the tempers of youngsters who've been involved in a fight.

For superintendents and board members, a prime example of mission-critical work is the board meeting. This meeting presents a unique opportunity for the governance team to take actions that support powerful teaching and learning. In fact, it is probably a good idea for superintendents and board members to ask themselves after every board meeting, "What did we do at this meeting to help our district achieve its educational mission?" More often than not, however, we hear a sense of frustration from superintendents and board members that board meetings are about everything *but* teaching and learning, and in fact detract from rather than support teaching and learning. It does not have to be that way!

In a discussion between leaders in two large urban school districts, one group talked with despair about the lack of support from their school board, the confusion about what they were expected to accomplish, and the toxic culture of their district. In contrast, the other district's leaders spoke of a board and superintendent who had limited the district to two goals: focus on the neediest students and examine how our teaching needs to change to help those students. These leaders knew what they were supposed to do, they felt supported, and they loved their work. The contrast between the two districts illustrates the point—make sure every person in the district knows the mission and sticks to it.

People pay attention to those in leadership positions. Knowing this is probably a good first step to creating board meetings that support teaching and learning. Why? Not because we have some exalted view of the role of the superintendent and board members, but because students closely observe their teachers' behavior in the classroom. They quickly note when teachers' actions are contrary to the very rules and guidelines they have established for student behavior. The message students receive is that the teacher is not really serious about the rules. "Do as I say, not as I do" rarely flies. Similarly, the way a principal or superintendent behaves in a potentially negative or hostile situation can make that situation much better or much worse. The same is true for board members—their behavior as well as the words they use during a board meeting speak volumes about what they truly value. For example, comments promoting self over team send a clear message that is contradictory to collaboration.

The fact of the matter is that superintendents and board members, like teachers and principals, are leaders. The work they do causes certain things to happen—or not happen, as the case may be. People are always watching what they do and comparing it to what they say. Superintendents and boards may say they believe all children can learn, but then they undo that belief by adopting a policy restricting access to rigorous classes for some students. The superintendent–board leadership team may want staff to treat students with respect, but if they do not treat each other or the public with respect, they send a clear message that "respect" simply is not a high value.

Position—that is, the title the leader holds—is important, and so are the leaders' abilities and skills that result in effective education leadership. That leadership is exhibited by teachers who lead and guide students, principals who set their schools moving in the right direction, superintendents who engage in systemic improvement efforts, and boards of education who set policies that give framework and structure to the education of children. But the superintendent–board leadership team sets the tone. How they do their work sets an example and influences people throughout the organization.

If the superintendent–board leadership team establishes a shared vision of excellence, stays focused on the right mission, builds people's capacity to do mission-critical work well, and reinforces cultural norms and core values that support high levels of achievement for all, so will the other people in the district. If the superintendent–board leadership team demonstrates that character and ethics are important, so will others. If the superintendent–board leadership team promotes continuous improvement, establishes good lines of communication, finds creative solutions to complex and enduring problems, practices collaboration, and models a culture of caring, then so will others who share responsibility for the education of children. Effective leaders make this a team sport, not an individual pursuit.

TEACHING AND LEARNING

Effective superintendents know a great deal about what promotes powerful teaching and learning. As an effective superintendent, you take advantage of every opportunity to demonstrate powerful teaching and learning. That includes board meetings and other interactions with the board, staff, students, and community. If you do so, you model the behavior you expect and you encourage principals and others to do the same. This is one of the essential leadership challenges in education: to build consistency in policy and practice throughout the district to promote and reinforce what we know to be the most likely to produce powerful teaching and learning experiences for children of all sizes, shapes, and colors.

That is why we believe board meetings present a unique opportunity for education leaders to come together to meet the leadership challenge. These board meetings are well covered by the media, discussed by staff and community, and are frequently the subject of editorials. In many communities, more attention is focused on the board meeting than any other single educational activity.

The sad fact is that these board meetings too often seem to operate in a world separate from that of teaching and learning. Little seems connected in some meaningful way to what is going on or should be going on in schools and classrooms. Instead of being seen as a wonderful opportunity to reinforce the district's mission and to support powerful teaching and learning, board meetings are seen as something to be endured, something to be survived, and something far removed from the district's core work. That need not be the case. Some of the successful experiences of superintendents and board members in communities across this country suggest how and why board meetings can connect to teaching and learning. We suggest ways in the following chapters.

Viewing board meetings as part of the larger context of a general and sometimes nebulous topic called "superintendent and board relations" misses the mark. They are instead an essential component of the district's overall effort to support powerful teaching and learning. Fundamentally, board meetings should focus on the question, "What are the practices we would like to see occurring in every classroom every day?" Thus, the leadership challenge for superintendents and board members is to ensure that their meetings encourage, model, support, and reward the kinds of powerful teaching and learning experiences the district wants to be part of every child's educational experience. That is why we believe that, for superintendents, the preparation for, conduct of, and follow-up from board meetings is mission-critical work.

Conversations among superintendents about board meetings, however, rarely convey a sense that these meetings are viewed as mission-critical activities. On the contrary, superintendents often view board meetings with anxiety and even a sense of dread. Most superintendents we know do their best to anticipate questions from board members, prepare for specific public communications—while knowing there may be a surprise or two here—and work with the media. Despite best efforts at preparation, it is almost impossible to control the specific events and circumstances that are likely to unfold.

We have often asked our colleagues in meetings of superintendents to tell us the top 10 signs that a board meeting is not going well. The list they generate includes an unanticipated presence of a large number of union representatives, a closed session called by the board president who then asks the superintendent to wait outside, or an angry citizen with a copy of his tax bill in hand. This activity is often humorous and draws laughs—unless, of course, you are the superintendent who happens to be the main character in the story. No wonder when we ask superintendents what they do to recover from board meetings, we get a list that would produce a great deal of comfort to those holding stocks in beverage or rich foods industries.

But control over what happens is not the only issue. Together, many board members and superintendents express frustration at the apparent disconnect between agendas of board meetings and the essential teaching and learning work of the school district. "What does this have to do with schools or the classroom?" is a common lament. "I wanted to make a difference for children," said one board member, "but much of what we do at board meetings seems more about adults than it does kids." The sad fact, of course, is that laments such as these reflect all too closely what actually happens.

Another factor to consider is that the public perception of education quality is shaped in part by its view of the board and superintendent in action. The public may know less about esoteric topics such as board–superintendent relations, but it does know when it sees people behaving badly or when the actions of the board do not seem to relate to education. The media, including television and the Internet in many cases, covers board meetings more than any other educational activity. One can only guess what opinions are formed about educational quality after citizens watch an acrimonious meeting, observe the topics that actually occupy board time and energy, and see people treat each other in ways they would not want their children treated in the classroom.

The public knows board members and superintendents are the education leaders of the community. What those leaders say and do reflects, for better or for worse, the norms and values of the school district. If we are dedicated to keeping citizens in public schools, it is to our advantage to create environments where everyone is supported in doing the right work for the right reasons. We must therefore prevent situations where our work, our employees, and our learners are unfairly challenged or maligned.

In a sense, the agenda for a board meeting is like a lesson plan. A good lesson has clearly stated learning objectives, carefully designed teaching strategies to help students meet the objectives, instructional materials to support teaching and learning, and a means of evaluating the extent to which learning actually occurred. Similarly, a good board meeting has an agenda that clearly articulates expected outcomes, has backup materials providing information needed to achieve the outcomes, has established processes that help board members consider input from others and discuss their different points of view, and has a way to evaluate the effectiveness of the meeting itself. As one board member expressed succinctly, "Did we do what we wanted to do and how do we know it?"

To this point, we have argued that the challenge for education leaders, including superintendents and board members, is to keep everyone focused on the right mission—providing all students with the powerful teaching and learning experiences that enable them to meet high standards. We have also stated our belief that effective board meetings are mission-critical; that is, they have the potential of impacting in a significant way the quality of teaching and learning in the school district. We believe we must help boards do their essential work in public and avoid creating a public forum that distracts the board from that work.

The leadership challenge for board members and superintendents is clear: make sure board meetings are driven by the district's teaching and learning mission. In the coming chapters, we will draw on the comments and successful practices of many of our colleagues, our own experiences and research, and some excellent work on governance and superintendent–board relations by the American Association of School Administrators (AASA), the National School Boards Association (NSBA), the California Schools Boards Association (CSBA), the Iowa School Boards Association, and a New England governance study, to see what we can do to ensure that board meetings reflect as well as drive the district's teaching and learning mission.

2

Building the Superintendent– Board Team

When you combine your personal commitment with respect for the commitment of others, you will initiate a compounding effect that will create a commitment to service throughout the organization.

(Nair, 1994, p. 81)

What if citizens from another country, who were interested in learning more about the relations between superintendents and board members in the United States, decided they could learn the most about the nature of these relationships not by reading the literature on the subject but by watching a variety of school board meetings? Then, wanting to verify their findings, they conducted a series of interviews with superintendents and board members.

What would they conclude? Judging by the conversations we have had with superintendents and board members over the years about board meetings, we think they are likely to conclude that the relations between members of both groups are sometimes strong and professional, but are often unclear and in fact tenuous and fragile.

If these conclusions are right, and we think they may be, there is a reason. Events leading up to and occurring at and after board meetings both reflect and define the nature of superintendent–board relations. Consequently, whatever we can do to improve the quality of board meetings is likely to have a favorable impact on superintendent–board relations.

Consider these examples. The decisions made about the kinds of items brought to the board for information, discussion, and action, speak volumes about the responsibilities of the board and the superintendent as CEO. If the board discusses trivial matters or if the board members offer their thoughts on topics appropriately considered to be "management" responsibilities, it is difficult to determine who is responsible for governance and who is responsible for management.

While it is often glibly stated that "boards make policies and the superintendent implements them," it seems there is often confusion over roles and responsibilities. For example, if the board were properly exercising its governance role, it would establish policies that guided the hiring of competent and qualified personnel. The superintendent would be responsible for the actual hiring and assignment for a specific position. Therefore, it is inappropriate for the board to discuss at which school, for example, the new vice principal will fit best.

At the board meeting itself, if the board reacts to "squeaky wheels" rather than thoughtfully prepared recommendations from superintendents or committees to the superintendent, or if the board engages in extensive discussion about a line item in the budget, what could one reasonably conclude about the role of the board? Do they govern? Or do they manage?

Picture this scene we actually witnessed at a school board meeting. The board is seated in a semicircle on a raised platform. The superintendent and staff are positioned on a level three feet below. Periodically, the board president or other member issues some sort of directive to the staff. The superintendent responds to that board member by indicating who will do what to follow up. What might a reasonable person conclude as to who is in charge of the organization and whether there is a CEO? If observers wanted to push an agenda or get a problem resolved, to whom should they go? What would an audience member who is considering running for the board in the future think was the appropriate role of a board member?

Contrast this kind of meeting with one where most of the board meeting is spent with the board reviewing progress toward goals in the district's strategic plan, making sure that sufficient funds are available to accomplish the goals, recognizing significant contributions of staff toward accomplishment of the district's mission, or evaluating the performance of the superintendent. In such a meeting, it is very clear who is responsible for governance and who is responsible for management. In the larger context of superintendent–board relations, the board meeting may be only one piece, but it is a big one. The adherence to appropriate roles by the board and superintendent, and the quality of the board meeting itself, influence significantly the nature of these relations.

DISTINCT AND COMPLEMENTARY ROLES

Because board meetings help define superintendent–board relations, we believe they must reflect and respect the differing roles of the board and superintendent. Board members and superintendents are leaders, and together they should constitute a leadership team, but they have different leadership responsibilities and ways to carry them out. The board is responsible for governance, the superintendent for management.

The term "management" is sometimes seen as different from leadership. "Are we leaders or managers?" a superintendent once asked us. Our response: "Yes to both." Good managers are good leaders. And good leaders are good managers. As "management leaders," superintendents provide leadership to the entire organization, deliver results expected by the board, and operate within policies established by the board exercising its governance role.

When the board is asked or expected to deal with management responsibilities in any area, lines of authority in the organization become blurred and the ability of the board to hold the superintendent accountable is diminished. That is in part why the board meeting and all that goes with it—preparation of the board agenda, the interactions at the meeting, the seating patterns at the meeting, follow-up from meetings, and more—all define overtly and covertly the functions of the board and superintendent.

We go a step further. Superintendent–board relations that respect the governance role of the board, the management role of the superintendent, and the leadership of both, are essential if the district is to achieve its teaching and learning mission. When the board–superintendent relationship sours or even when it is not functioning the way it should, the ability of the leadership team to stay focused on teaching and learning is diminished. As John Carver (1997) writes in *Boards That Make a Difference*, "No single relationship in the organization is as important as that between the Board and its CEO. . . . That relationship, well conceived, can set the stage for effective governance and management" (p. 101).

Carver's work is consistent with the findings of an excellent study on school governance by Richard Goodman, Luann Fulbright, and William O. Zimmerman, Jr. The authors identify policies and practices that contribute to a strong superintendent–board leadership team that focuses on student achievement (Goodman et al., 1997). These findings are reflected in the governance standards developed by the California School Board Association (CSBA), and support the continuing work of the American Association of School Administrators (AASA) and National School Boards Association (NSBA) on effective governance.

Collectively, these works agree that both the board and the superintendent have critical leadership roles, but they exercise these in different ways—the board through governance, the superintendent through management. The former establishes policies, which the latter carries out as the chief executive officer. If each exercises its particular leadership role in a responsible manner, the organization functions much more effectively. The ability to achieve the district's mission is significantly enhanced. Why? Carver (1997) is again helpful:

- A powerfully designed CEO position is a key to board excellence. It enables a board to avoid the intricacies and short-term focus of staff management and to work exclusively on the holistic, long-term focus of governance (p. 102).
- The board's relationship with the CEO is formed around the accountability of the position, not its responsibility. . . . The board's concern is confined to what it holds the CEO accountable for (p. 106).
- Boards caught in the trap of being better staff than staff and boards bewildered by unending details or confused by technical complexities cannot lead. A modern approach to governance must enable a board to cut quickly to the heart of an organization (p. 22).

The board's role is to set the direction for the district, identify expected results, request information that enables it to determine whether the expected results are achieved, and define the relationship between the board and superintendent. Much of this is accomplished through its policymaking role, a function that should be at the forefront of each board meeting agenda.

We recommend you review several of your district's board agendas to see whether the board's time is occupied establishing, reviewing, or updating policies that focus on results; defining parameters within which the superintendent is expected to operate; and reviewing information necessary for the board to exercise its governance function. If the board is focusing on these activities at the board meeting, it is likely you and your board are working together as an effective leadership team, each respecting your appropriate roles. If the agenda reflects mostly administrative issues and concerns, you have the power and indeed the responsibility to change the agenda.

As superintendent, the chief executive officer, you work within the policies established by your board. You exercise your leadership role through these policies. If the policies are creating problems in areas such as the hiring or evaluation of staff; financial management; implementation of an effective organizational structure; or the alignment of curriculum, instruction, and assessment, then it is time for you to recommend changes in policy. The answer is not for you and the board to start interfering with the ability of both parties to carry out their governance and management responsibilities, but rather to take the time to review, discuss, and commit to appropriate roles.

POLICY-DRIVEN MEETINGS

The board meeting's impact on board–superintendent relations lies in the fact that the meeting is the vehicle through which each party demonstrates and meets its obligations to the leadership team. When you give careful attention to planning the agenda and the agenda items, you make it easier for both you and the board to pay conscious attention to your respective leadership roles. Discussion of and action on policies should occupy the majority of the board's attention.

This does not exclude other items such as the need for the board to exercise its representative function with constituents. Listening to the community and working with it to shape the direction of the district in a way that supports powerful teaching and learning is critical to the board, superintendent, and district's success. However, the board meeting is the actual time when the board properly exercises its governance responsibilities.

Using most of board meeting time to deal with policy issues respects and acknowledges the important governance functions for which the board is responsible. Carver (1997) makes the point well: "Because policies permeate and dominate all aspects of organizational life, they present the most powerful lever for the exercise of leadership" (p. 25).

Effective policies establish direction for the district and superintendent in a wide variety of areas including curriculum, instruction, assessment, student support services, human resources, business services, and facilities. They should deal with results, parameters within which staff is expected to operate, board–staff relations, and processes by which the board represents its constituency, provides strategic leadership and monitors progress toward goals. As superintendent, you then provide the information the board requires to do its job well and make recommendations for action when appropriate.

If you or members of the board choose to "load the agenda" with discussions and actions that are in essence not directly related to the board's governance responsibilities, the board's ability to do its mission-critical work well is impacted adversely. It is far better for a board meeting to be shorter and focus on the right things than longer and filled with matters that more appropriately fall within the superintendent's range of responsibilities. We reiterated that, since agenda planning is the superintendent's role, you take the lead to make sure the agenda furthers the board's role to govern, not manage. A board meeting should not appear to be a staff meeting with the board seemingly directing the daily work of the superintendent and the staff.

Stating that board meetings should reflect the appropriate governance and management roles of superintendents and boards is one thing; doing it is quite another. But there are two useful ways for the superintendent–board leadership team to translate perspectives on governance and management into action. The first is your commitment to developing a board agenda that is focused on mission-critical work. The second is to actually plan each board agenda so it is focused on the mission-critical teaching and learning work of the district (Goodman et al., 1997). If, as the authors recommend, boards and superintendents attend to vision, structure, accountability, advocacy, and unity, they will function as effective leadership teams that stay focused on this mission-critical work of student achievement. Because commitment to mission drives everything else, we will look at that first.

Mission

When we consider the roles and responsibilities of boards and superintendents, we look at what each does to enable the district to achieve its mission and how board meetings either support or inhibit that work. The board through its policies and processes clearly defines the mission and monitors progress toward that mission. The superintendent articulates the mission to staff and community and takes the actions necessary to make sure the mission is accomplished.

We believe every board meeting should include acknowledgment of successful mission-critical activities within the district, discussions or actions that enable the district to accomplish its mission, and/or the monitoring of progress toward achievement of the mission. The board meeting itself is mission-critical—or at least it should be. It is one of the most important opportunities to articulate to students, staff, and community exactly what the district is all about and what is being done to educate all the students well. If the agenda does not acknowledge the importance of this critical work, what is the message sent to the community?

Schools are institutions of teaching and learning. If learning is the product, then teaching is the means to ensure that learning occurs. As superintendent, it is your role to educate the board as to the conditions and activities necessary if learning is to occur. The board through its governance role does its best to encourage, provide, and reward these conditions and activities. All board members and the superintendent need to be absolutely clear as to the characteristics of powerful teaching and learning and then model those in their work.

Whatever we want to happen in the classroom and schools should be modeled at the board meeting. Activities inhibiting powerful teaching and learning should be avoided and eliminated. As an example, we know that properly done, learning in groups can improve student achievement. Board meetings, then, should reflect what we know about positive group-learning conditions. We also know that learning occurs when people discover something they did not know before. Usually this happens as a result of a "listening" experience—especially when it introduces a perspective that might be new. Do board meetings reflect a willingness to listen and respect different viewpoints? We hope so. How the board listens, considers, and discusses sends a message about the value its members place on teaching and learning. Our belief is that just like superintendents, board members are learners as well as teachers and will model this at the board meeting.

The New England Governance Study, *Getting There From Here* (Goodman, 1997), provides us with thoughtful perspectives on how board meetings might stay focused on this mission-critical work. While they are intended to guide relations between the superintendent and board in general, the concepts of vision, structure, accountability, advocacy, and unity may be used as a framework for agenda planning and board meeting conduct. We will look at each to see how it might be useful in this regard.

Vision

The superintendent and board, with input from others, develop a vision of a high-performing district. What will it look like around here if everyone—students and staff—is achieving at a high level? Vision is important because it defines direction. It helps maintain an important sense of focus in districts where there is a constant tug to add more and more to the plate or undertake one innovation after another. We recommend that at least four board meetings a year be devoted to a vision-related discussion. Strategic planning includes environmental scanning, assessing needs, and goal setting. Each of these is an important component of the vision discussion. This discussion, by the way, also affords a unique opportunity to get staff and community involved in charting the direction of the district and in building support and understanding of the teaching and learning mission.

Structure

Every organization needs to have a system in place to help it move toward its vision and accomplish mission-critical work. That system is the structure of the organization—namely the policies, plans, processes, and human, fiscal, and physical resources that encourage growth and improvement. Almost every board meeting should have one or more structure-related topics on the agenda. However, a word of caution: The structure discussions must be related to the board's governance responsibilities, not the superintendent's management responsibilities. Examples in personnel and finance are instructive.

In the area of personnel, the board's job is to establish policies that help the district hire and maintain high-quality staff. Working conditions, compensation, and expectations for professional development and evaluation arc all appropriate policy areas for the board. But there is a big difference between saying the board expects evaluation of staff performance to be done and engaging in that activity itself. The latter is clearly the responsibility of the superintendent, who cannot and should not be held accountable for staff performance without the authority to conduct evaluation. When the board takes on the superintendent's job, it weakens the entire accountability system. The exception, of course, is the evaluation of the superintendent and the board's evaluation of itself. Both are board responsibilities.

Finance is also an important governance responsibility. The board should have policies in place that guide and regulate such practices as bidding, purchasing, auditing, and protecting reserves and fund balances. To exercise this responsibility, the board must receive accurate and reliable financial information from the superintendent. The board should also establish budget priorities, make sure these priorities are aligned to the vision and strategic goals, and work to ensure resources are allocated to these priorities. As a wise superintendent once reminded a board, "A goal without resources is not a goal, it is an illusion." Planning and conducting the board meeting so the board can exercise its fiduciary responsibilities under the law is critical. The board's job is not to engage in discussions of line items in the budget such as the telephone bill. Remember, when the board is spending time on items it should not, it is not spending time on items it should.

Accountability

A good way to think about accountability is through a process called "the cycle of inquiry." This process is data driven. Information is gathered from a variety of sources and is used to develop both strategic long- and short-term goals. Superintendents and boards then work together as a leadership team to set targets and identify indicators to track progress toward reaching the goals. These indicators are then used to determine what is working well and where improvements are needed. As a result, new goals may be set.

When it is working well, the cycle of inquiry clearly establishes who is accountable for what. At the board meeting, for example, the board and superintendent together review data that indicate the extent to which established goals and indicators are being met. Completed goals are celebrated and removed from the list. Existing goals are refined and new goals added. Responsibility for achieving the goals is assigned to the superintendent who in turn directs the work of the staff to meet goals and report on indicators of progress. The superintendent and staff also identify barriers to success and plan for improvement. The superintendent communicates progress on the plan to the board. This report of progress and achievement would constitute the fundamental basis for the superintendent's evaluation.

To keep the focus on teaching and learning, we suggest that student achievement and the conditions which support it, such as a high-quality teaching staff, sufficient resources, and a strong leadership team, become the basis for the cycle of inquiry in general and accountability in particular. We believe every board meeting should include items on the agenda that have something to do with the efforts of the superintendent and board to strengthen student achievement, whether it is goal setting, allocation of resources, or evaluation of progress toward established goals. In that sense, accountability is not an annual event involving the superintendent's evaluation or the board's assessment of itself, but an ongoing activity that sends a message that data-driven accountability is how we do things around here.

Advocacy

Board meetings provide an opportunity for boards and superintendents to advocate for the cause of public education. When that occurs, the public understands that the board–superintendent team is united in the belief that public education is the vehicle for helping all students irrespective of race, ethnicity, religion, or socioeconomic status meet high standards. The advocacy role includes reporting on interactions with legislators or having elected officials come to the meeting. This is a good opportunity for the legislators, the board, and you to promote policies and practices that improve opportunities for all students.

Other advocacy actions include acknowledgments and recognitions of individual and group accomplishments and inviting presentations from schools and community groups. Time for a report from each individual board member, a section that appears on many board agendas, too often provides an excuse to bring up topics that are not on the agenda. Instead, work with the board to report on efforts to influence legislation, communicate with the community, and promote partnerships and alliances with the public and private sectors.

Unity

The board meeting is an opportunity for staff and community to watch interactions between the board and superintendent. If the community sees the board and superintendent working together to move toward achievement of the district's vision, honoring their respective governance and management roles, and doing mission-critical work, it is far more likely to have confidence in the district's leadership. The purpose is not to eliminate conflict or disagreement. In fact, it works to the betterment of the system if the public knows that decisions are made after consideration of different perspectives and thorough discussion. We agree with those who advocate that we should be tough on the issues, but soft on the people.

Modeling what we expect to occur in every classroom and school should be the guiding principle. In that sense, the leadership team should model effective problem-solving and conflict-resolution strategies, keeping personal interest and ego in check. As Goethe said, "Things which matter most should never be at the mercy of things which matter least." The welfare of students always comes first.

While we recognize that state laws require boards to approve a wide variety of actions, those pertaining to vision, structure, accountability, advocacy, and unity matter the most. These five concepts are one set of criteria by which boards and superintendents can evaluate the effectiveness of board meetings.

In summary, we suggest that for board meetings to build a strong foundation for the accomplishment of district goals and demonstrate a positive, united superintendent–board leadership team, they must do the following:

- Have an agenda that respects the leadership roles of board members and superintendents, but differentiates between the governance role of the board and the executive officer responsibilities of the superintendent.
- Develop and maintain steady, unrelenting focus on the mission and what it takes to accomplish that mission.
- Model the principles of good teaching and learning.
- Use the guiding principles of vision, structure, accountability, advocacy, and unity to keep the board and superintendent focused on the unique responsibilities of each and function as a high-achieving leadership team.

PART II

Pre-Meeting Planning

Effective superintendents look at board meetings as one of their most important work products. They leave to chance only that which truly is chance. The simple fact is effective meetings start with thorough, and detailed, pre-meeting planning.

Think about what exceptional teachers do in preparing a lesson plan. They plan their lessons carefully and with student outcomes in mind. They prepare their rooms and materials to support lessons to achieve their goals. Delivery of effective lessons requires clear communication as the teacher helps students learn and understand the concepts and facts.

Effective superintendents do the same in planning for board meetings. They pay careful attention to each of four critical areas:

- Planning the agenda and individual agenda items
- Setting pre-meeting arrangements
- Designing the board packet and backup information
- Communicating the agenda with board members and others

Multiple options are available. The ones the superintendent chooses can either improve the likelihood of an effective meeting or create additional obstacles hindering the superintendent and board in doing their best work as they carry out their leadership responsibilities. Stories of bad board meetings abound, often told by unemployed superintendents.

Although board members, particularly the board president, are actively involved in planning the meeting agenda, in most cases the superintendent has the responsibility for planning the board meeting. We think the board meeting agenda and packet are the superintendent's best work on public display, and must reflect the importance of quality teaching and learning.

Planning the overall agenda is the focus of Chapter 3 and includes a number of important aspects. The 12-month calendar is a useful planning tool and keeps everyone focused on the major district goals. Other important topics are the activities of the planning team in developing the overall agenda, and the individual agenda items and whether to present the board with an information and/or action item. Some topics are better handled in settings other than the regular, formal board meeting and these include a special meeting, town hall or open forum, study session, or board workshop.

A superintendent or board member new to a district inherits tradition related to the board meeting—frequency of meetings, day and time, and location. They also inherit subtler aspects such as room arrangements and ambience, where the board and superintendent sit, and treatment of the audience. There are choices about handling each of these that we will discuss in Chapter 4. In addition, we offer suggestions for minimizing the chance of the unexpected and ways to respond to an unusual turn of events—a perennial concern of superintendents.

While traditions regarding processes for board packet preparation also may be in place, a new superintendent has the advantage of reviewing these processes with "fresh eyes." While we never encourage anyone to change simply for change's sake, we do think superintendents need to look at the effectiveness of the current system, recognizing the balance between preserving the best of the past while making needed improvements. This is another component of leadership.

Chapter 5 covers the design of the board packet itself. The board packet assists the board at the meeting, and serves as an important communications document. Therefore the packet must reflect quality in thinking, planning, direction, and appearance, reflecting the same high standards we expect from a great lesson. We recognize outstanding teachers for their ability to create and deliver great lessons. As superintendents, we are obligated to present our work using the same high standards and level of professionalism.

We include ideas for the overall look of the agenda, the cover of the document, the table of contents and/or summary page, the agenda item format, and other considerations about which we think you must make specific decisions. We will also remind you here and in Chapter 3: Do not forget to proofread!

Communicating with key people and groups regarding the agenda and specific items is the final critical step except for making last-minute adjustments as situations arise. In Chapter 6, we suggest options, and cautions, for communicating with board members, the staff, other stakeholders, and the media. Ideally, the superintendent's communications efforts will result in the highest level of preparation of stakeholders to create effectiveness and efficiency and reduce surprises.

Taken together, and connected to the overall district mission, efficient and effective planning will enhance the quality of the board meeting. You may not receive praise for a good meeting, but critics will quickly pounce on any evidence of poor planning, illegal posting of items, missed timelines, grammatical errors, and erroneous information.

In the spirit of continuous improvement, we encourage new and experienced superintendents to reevaluate periodically the effectiveness and efficiency of all practices related to preparing for the board meeting, no matter how long their tenure in a district, because times and circumstances change. Reviewing and improving practices pays off in increased productivity and accomplishment of our mission.

3

Planning the Calendar and Agenda

As the lesson plan guides the classroom teacher, the board meeting agenda is the centerpiece of effective board meetings. The agenda is the work product of the superintendent.

(Johnston et al., 2002, p. 50)

The primary goal of superintendents and boards is to foster high-quality teaching and learning that improves student achievement. This goal should guide the preparation of the overall agenda and all agenda items so that the board meeting models the best in teaching and learning.

To that end, everything on the agenda must support the district's teaching and learning mission. For some agenda items, the link to the district's mission and short- and long-range goals will be obvious. For others, the link may be less direct but nonetheless they are part of the board's mission-critical work. Expending funds, honoring students for specific achievement, or approving personnel items, should all contribute to the goal of improving the achievement of every student.

Agenda planning processes are iterative—that is, although development processes flow in a sequence, they often circle back and forth on each other. Each step leads to a refinement of the ideas, the presentation, the writing itself, or the ultimate action the board will be asked to accomplish at each meeting.

In this chapter, we present planning ideas for four main topics: the 12-month calendar, the regular board meeting agenda, individual agenda items, and special meetings of various types. Whether preparing for regular or special meetings, superintendents start with thinking about the big picture and work to ensure the details support the ultimate goals.

Every meeting, regardless of type and purpose, requires planning. The superintendent decides what meetings to hold, when to hold them, and whom to involve. Planning meetings are routine, regular occurrences. Periodically, it is useful to take time to assess their effectiveness with an eye to continuous improvement.

TWELVE-MONTH CALENDAR

Planning starts with the long-range view of topics the board will likely consider over the school year. A good way to develop this long-range view is to create a 12-month agenda calendar of projected board meeting agenda topics. We will use the shortened term, 12-month calendar.

Description

First, let's clarify what the 12-month calendar is and is not. It is a big-picture document created to provide a snapshot of the year's significant events and issues the board will address. Ideally, it is formatted to fit on one piece of paper. Board members, superintendent, and staff may then refer to this one-page overview on an ongoing basis to prepare meeting agendas and individual agenda items for the board of trustees.

Two general categories of items make up a board meeting agenda. First are the infrequent and high-priority ones, and second, the routine items addressing the day-to-day business of the district. As Stephen Covey, author of *Seven Habits of Highly Effective People*, among others, has stressed, it is critical to work on the important issues, and clarify the difference between important and urgent and important and *not* urgent (Covey, 1990), both of which are important for the operation of the district. The calendar does not need all the items for the year, but should capture high-priority topics. If it is necessary to include routine topics, they could be grouped and summarized in major categories such as business and personnel. A district operating without the planning calendar is by implication stating that board meetings are spontaneous occurrences where unanticipated events are expected. Surprises happen even with the calendar, but creating an environment that minimizes the chance of chaos is the goal. (Please see Resource B, p. 151.)

AUDIENCE

The 12-month calendar will serve multiple constituencies: the board, superintendent, staff, public, and media.

First, it helps the superintendent plan effectively and prevent important items from falling through the cracks. When a new issue comes up—a new state mandate, or a desire by a board member for a report—the superintendent looks at the calendar to determine where and when the new item fits in the year's work, or if it should. Of course, not every issue that comes to a school district belongs on the board agenda. The 12-month calendar is also a tool the superintendent may use to avoid loading up any one agenda with too many difficult issues, and instead spread them out so the board can deal with items in a more reasoned and thoughtful manner. It is a process of focus and priority setting, and a way to ensure that most of the board meetings deal with teaching and learning throughout the year.

There is a fringe benefit as well. When interest in a new topic develops, the calendar becomes a vehicle superintendents can use to remind board members of the impact on existing staff responsibilities that are aligned to the calendar and established board priorities. Superintendents use the graphic display of year-long plans to show how adding a new project impacts already-planned activities. Adding something new may cause planned goals and activities to be dropped, or timelines shifted.

Second, the calendar provides an opportunity for individual board members to suggest topics for consideration and for the full board to prioritize those items. Staying focused increases a district's effectiveness. Board members can see how a potential new topic fits—or does not fit—into the overall district plan and interests of their colleagues.

Thus, when a board member returns from a conference with a new—and often very good—idea or program to benefit students, there is a filter in place to evaluate the immediate importance of this item. This happened one night at a meeting we observed. After the board member described the program and the great results other districts received, there was silence. Finally, another board member said, "Well, that sounds very good. But if we add this program, what will we need to drop from our existing plan for the year?" To the originating board member's credit, the reply was, "Oops, I think maybe this should go on our list of potential ideas for next year's planning."

We know some boards have a member who frequently wants to place the latest hot issue on the agenda. While the topics may need attention, they are not necessarily items for the agenda. The 12-month calendar helps maintain the integrity of the agenda against "pop-up" special-interest items.

Third, for the staff, the 12-month calendar provides a guide for planning their work schedules. A useful practice is for staff members to develop their own 12-month calendar. They create their own timelines based first on the districtwide 12-month calendar, adding their own high-priority goals, and finally the routine daily, weekly, and monthly tasks falling within their area of responsibility. This practice also aids in keeping staff on track at meetings. As Tom Peters (1982) says, "We stick to the knitting" (p. 292).

Finally, the 12-month calendar serves as an important vehicle for communication with the public and media. Looking at the 12-month calendar, parents, interested citizens, and members of the media can see the district's priorities and the breadth of issues the board and staff deal with over the course of a year. Parents and other citizens can look ahead to areas of particular interest for them. The media appreciate the calendar because it provides potential story topics and the opportunity to do advanced research. While there are happy people who go to the market without a list or on vacation without an itinerary, these shoppers and travelers tend to spend more, experience frustration, and end up less satisfied. We think the same happens with unplanned board meetings.

Developers

The creator of the 12-month calendar often depends on the size of the district. In all instances however, the superintendent is the lead and determines whom to involve in the planning. Board members are always involved, but at different points in the process, and to varying degrees, depending on the superintendent's recommendations and the board's wishes.

Besides the size of the district, who participates in the creation of the calendar depends on tradition and the superintendent's assessment of whose knowledge and viewpoint will enhance planning. The calendar is the plan to *schedule* the work, not *do* the work. Inclusion of others assists in determining who does the work and when the work gets done; the calendar functions as a guide and reminder.

Here is an example of a how you might proceed with the annual calendar development. You prepare a draft of the calendar alone or in concert with the key leadership team (i.e., assistant superintendents and/or principals and department heads), often called the cabinet. Next you send the draft to other stakeholder groups for input. Stakeholder groups may include the broader leadership team, leaders of employee groups, and involved parent groups such as the PTA or educational foundation.

The calendar draft then goes to the board at a board meeting for its review, discussion, and input. This is a good time to see whether individual members have other topics to suggest. Ultimately, the board is in charge of the agenda, so their questions, suggestions, and recommendations are critical.

The final step is board adoption of the calendar with the caveat that the calendar is a living, planning document subject to modification as situations warrant, without the necessity of the board officially readopting the calendar as changes are made.

No hard and fast rules exist. The calendar reflects the varieties of leadership styles, traditions of practices, and choices to improve effectiveness. For example, some superintendents find it effective to include representatives of various groups such as the leaders of employee groups and parent organizations, along with a representative or two from the school board, in the original planning meeting.

A wonderful resource is the superintendent's administrative assistant who can go back through the past two years of board meeting agendas and note those items and topics occurring at the same time each year.

Process

In creating the calendar, think about the district's mission and strategic or long-range plan, which we will call the "district plan." As mission-critical work, the district plan specifies the district's major goals and objectives and drives the work of the superintendent and district staff. The superintendent should be evaluated based in large part on the achievement of or progress toward accomplishment of these goals.

Since achievement of goals results from the work of the total district team, successful superintendents expect the staff to focus on the district plan. Therefore the key leaders establish goals within their areas of responsibility. For example, a district may set a goal of increasing the racial and gender diversity of the district's administrators and teachers, because its leadership believes a staff that reflects the diversity of the student population will have a positive effect on student success. If so, the head of human resources working with the superintendent sets targets and plans activities to achieve this goal.

The superintendent and planning group determine timelines for benchmarks of progress or accomplishment of each district goal, and from these decides when reports will go to the board for information, discussion, and/or action. The team puts these dates on the calendar.

Also include on the calendar those significant annual activities and tasks that tend to occur at or about the same time each year and have major implications for the district. For example, after district or state student test results are available, staff prepares a report of findings and analysis of strengths and weaknesses. Determine when the testing reports will go to the board and put those dates on the calendar.

After assessing whether each is truly an annual item, put it on the draft 12-month calendar. For example, the budget for the coming year tends to be introduced about the same time annually. In some states, this is after the state announces its preliminary budget; in others, the first budget discussion follows a city or county release of the budget forecast, or a referendum to levy taxes. Some districts handle the budget adoption in one step; others have a two-step budget adoption process. If you have a two-step process, both the date of the introduction of the budget and the date of the adoption go on the calendar.

Personnel notifications are often regulated by district, county, or state mandates. Since legal dates for notifying staff that they may not be returning the next year are critical, related actions must be on the 12-month calendar. Also, some grants must be renewed at a particular time. If so, place these at the appropriate place on the calendar.

Staff is responsible for many other items. Some are a matter of law or district practice, are routine, and go to the board monthly. The responsible person must see that these items are submitted for the appropriate board meeting, but they do *not* need to go on the 12-month calendar because of their routine nature. Examples include monthly pay warrants, purchase orders, the personnel register, and approval of travel and conference attendance.

Many districts schedule student, staff, and/or school and department recognitions and presentations at each meeting, or some of the meetings. Putting these dates on the calendar allows the superintendent to spread them out over the year so no one meeting is overloaded.

An example of the usefulness of the 12-month calendar is planning for a controversial issue, such as school attendance boundary changes. Typically, a district establishes a boundary committee whose charge is to look at various options and make recommendations to the board. Boundary changes provoke considerable emotion so it is wise to plan for either a separate hearing, or at the very least a discussion at one meeting and action at a second meeting. Note on the calendar each date when information or a request for action on boundary changes will go to the board. Some savvy superintendents make sure a student presentation or recognition of student achievement precedes a hot topic. This gives the audience a subtle reminder that regardless of the issue, students are the priority.

Appearance

Our advice is to make the calendar as straightforward and simple as possible to get the job done. The idea is to do the work, not develop complicated planning documents. The ideal adopted 12-month calendar is a one-page document, typically beginning with July and continuing to the following June, the school district's fiscal year. You can include this one-page document in each board packet, and people can carry it in their daily planner or briefcase. In addition, the superintendent's office and the board meeting room are great places for displaying the 12-month calendar. The calendar needs to be simple—if it is too complex, it will create yet another useless document just sitting in the district office.

Although the calendar may be board adopted, inevitably there will need to be modifications. Therefore it is important to note the date of the latest revision on the calendar itself so everyone is working from the same document.

The 12-month calendar can be structured in various ways, and there is excellent software available to make calendar development and revision simple. One method is to make a matrix with the months on one axis and the topics/items by department on the other. Or the topics/items may be listed by month and by categories such as main items, awards and recognitions, closed session, and special topics. Some items will appear twice—once when they are introduced for discussion, and a second time when the board will act on them. Another useful practice is noting the dates of special meetings or study sessions.

As with all tools, it is advisable to try a system and later evaluate its effectiveness. Does the structure enhance planning or would modifications make it more useful? Is it an effective communication and planning device and one that builds confidence of the staff and public in the ability of the district to address important topics? Used properly, the 12-month calendar is another tool for the superintendent and board to educate staff and community about teaching and learning and student achievement.

THE AGENDA PLANNING TEAM

Planning well is the first step in creating a successful lesson or meeting. Planning the agenda for a board meeting is especially critical. While a teacher often develops lesson plans alone or with a small group, as superintendent you think of the board meeting objectives and whom you want to involve. Some staff may be involved directly in the planning of the agenda; others will be involved at the reviewing stage. Regardless of how you do it, we believe it is essential for you to hold a planning meeting as an integral part of preparing each board agenda.

In addition to involving key staff members to help develop the agenda, you can use the planning meeting as a dress rehearsal for the actual board meeting. Here is a good time to anticipate likely questions from board members along with staff and community reaction to various agenda topics. While the outcome of a controversial item might not be predicted in advance, it is certain that being cavalier about planning, or not allocating enough time for planning, is a setup for disaster. A scene to avoid is the board president turning to the superintendent in the meeting and saying, "Why didn't we know about this?" The planning team is an ensemble cast. They rehearse together and support each other in the final production.

A former superintendent tells the story of arriving at a school board meeting without having attended the agenda-planning meeting due to the crush of other meetings she was facing in her large urban school district. As she glanced through the agenda, she noted a highly controversial item listed "for discussion," one she did not expect and had not talked with individual board members about, leaving them unprepared as well.

Naturally, members of the media had already seen the agenda and were ready for the kill, so even pulling the item off the agenda could not stop the onslaught. The result was months of national press and the diversion of energy and attention away from the students. Clearly, superintendents who come unprepared to meetings do so at their own peril.

Participants

Regardless of the size of the district, people meet to plan and organize the agenda for the upcoming meeting. In a small district, the planning team may consist of only the superintendent and secretary or administrative assistant. A mid-size district team may have key district office administrators and perhaps school site leaders working with the superintendent. In mid-size to large districts, superintendents often involve the heads of each division, e.g., business, educational services, special education, human resources, and others, including representatives of various management positions and presidents of employee associations and parent groups.

Not only does the size of the district influence which persons and how many are involved in the planning, but who attends the planning meetings is also a matter of purpose. Who, because of their role and responsibilities, must be at the meeting? And who could add value in thinking through items of importance?

What about the role of the board president? Some presidents like to be actively involved; others prefer to let the superintendent and staff handle the preparation and have the superintendent check with them on relatively few matters. In other districts, both the president and vice president are involved in planning.

Who from the board is involved and to what degree is a matter if not for board approval, at least for board knowledge. It is important that you ensure that all board members understand the role of the board in agenda planning.

When considering whom to include, superintendents think about the time commitment required, the expertise or viewpoint represented, and/or the "stake" others have in the items on the agenda. As an example, we know districts where school administrators, parents, and representatives from parent groups and unions participate in the planning session. When this occurs, we suggest the same representative attend each meeting to assure continuity and build a degree of comfort, for it contributes to open dialogue. We also stress the importance of scheduling the meeting at a time when all parties can attend.

Ultimately, the composition of the planning group is both practical and political. The superintendent decides the composition of the group and delineates clearly for all members the roles and expectations for participation. Keep in mind that increasing involvement of different parties does not diminish the superintendent's responsibility for the final product—the agenda—and the board meeting itself.

The Superintendent's Role

Our belief is that the superintendent is always a teacher. Superintendents who view planning meetings through this lens of teaching and learning suggest the inclusion of participants who can contribute directly and also act as communicators back to their respective constituencies.

The superintendent is also a learner, gaining insight from the various perspectives the participants bring. Other stakeholders are our teachers, not our adversaries. The more we understand the views of others through open dialogue, the more likely we are to produce quality information and build broad-based support for district goals.

Modeling is a powerful teacher. Superintendents who ask for criticism and alternative views, and then jump on someone who presents a contrary perspective, teach the lesson well—honesty and openness are not valued. Superintendents who are sincere about wanting honest dialogue, set the tone by encouraging, and then honoring and thanking those who offer a different voice. Isn't that what we want happening in every classroom?

An illustrative example is one that former South African president Nelson Mandela gives in his autobiography, *Long Road to Freedom.* Mr. Mandela had a conversation with a colonel about creating and leading a liberation army. The colonel told Mr. Mandela that when off duty one must "conduct yourself on the basis of perfect equality, even with the lowliest soldier. You must eat what they eat; you must not take your food in your office, but eat with them, drink with them, not isolate yourself" (Mandela, 1994, p. 306).

While Mandela was thinking this was admirable advice, a soldier came in to ask the colonel a question, to which the colonel responded, "Can't you see that I am talking to an important individual here? Don't you know not to interrupt me when I am eating? Now get out of my sight." The lesson was not in the words, but in the action. From the style of planning to the demeanor at the meeting, you are watched and are a symbol for the school district.

Planning Group Role

All members, while representing their organization or department's perspective, are also asked to look at the short- and long-term good of the whole district. Each person plays the "friendly critic" or "devil's advocate," asking probing questions and offering varying perspectives.

A special note must be made regarding the role of the superintendent's secretary or administrative assistant. Most often, it is the assistant who must prepare and assemble the actual agenda and meeting packet of information. The assistant's participation in the planning meeting is invaluable. The careful selection, training, and supervision of this important person are crucial tasks for the superintendent. The assistant takes notes, picks up important nuances about items and issues, is fully informed about the upcoming meeting, and answers questions and provides information for staff and others who call. This assistant is also the person on the telephone, or going into staff members' offices, asking for items to complete the packet. Assistants deeply appreciate superintendents who insist everyone meet deadlines.

The superintendent sets the tone and parameters for the planning group by describing the group's role. This is an essential step in ensuring the group is effective and efficient. In the process, the superintendent asks the group to look for areas that are unclear, controversial, or complicated. View this meeting both as dress rehearsal and an opportunity to train and support your staff.

Typically, the planning group thinks through all the items on the agenda, with the focus being on the non-routine items. To do this, the planning group, at a minimum, must have the title and brief description of each item. How detailed agenda items and reports are for the planning meeting is a function of the timeline established for staff to prepare reports. The superintendent makes clear what items are planned for the meeting, who is responsible for writing each agenda item, who must review the item, and what the timeline is for each of these activities.

In some cases, individual items may be thoroughly developed before they are brought to the planning meeting; at other times, perhaps just the key ideas are presented. The planning group's discussion can analyze what is presented or can help flesh out, if necessary and appropriate, background and summary information, options with pros and cons, and a recommendation for the board's consideration. This discussion helps the superintendent and the originator of the agenda item think through how the topic should be presented and what questions need to be answered. The thoroughness of this planning meeting helps not only in writing the final agenda item, but is an important education and communication tool for planning-team members.

Some districts list specific times for certain agenda items, indicating at what time during the meeting the board plans to discuss or take action on a topic. Others designate a few critical items as "time certain." Be cautious of listing an unrealistic time. The busy person who comes for the 7:00 p.m. item is not going to be happy at 9:00 p.m. when finally the item is presented.

For example, a board may wish to discuss a major contract with a new office and classroom supply company at a specific time, so next to the agenda item, it says 6:30 p.m. One more important reason boards use "time certain" is if paid consultants or attorneys will be present. This reduces the waiting time and therefore the cost to the district. In practice, the board should finish whatever item it is currently discussing at 6:30, and then take up the supply contract even if there are items preceding it on the agenda. After the time-certain item, the board returns to the previous place on the agenda.

Additional issues for the planning group may be the timing of recognitions and the length of presentations of programs and/or reports to the board. If audio-visual equipment will be required, the person responsible for setup is notified of what items are needed and when. That person's job is to make sure everything is tested and in working order prior to the start of the meeting. We know the stress caused by lengthy and poorly planned presentations, faulty technology, and random comments. We also know of unemployed superintendents who did not heed the advice to plan the meetings as their best lesson.

The wise superintendent makes sure a presenter knows the planned length of a presentation. We all have witnessed people who, when given a microphone, are reluctant to give it up. Therefore the superintendent directs presenters to rehearse their presentations beforehand, and to stay within the given time limit.

Planning meetings are very important for agenda items coming before the board for a first and second reading. The first reading means the board will consider the item and discuss it, but not take any action. The second reading is when the board takes up the item at the next or subsequent meeting for additional discussion and action. We do not recommend "fast tracking" items except in emergency situations. If an issue comes up that requires immediate action, be sure to check your state's laws about how quickly you can post the agenda and hold the meeting.

In the case of items going to the board for a second reading, the report from the first meeting can be reviewed at the planning meeting and discussed from the vantage point of questions and issues the board, and perhaps members of the public, raised at the first reading. The discussion often leads to a revision of the item for the board's second consideration.

Examples of items warranting discussion at one meeting (or more) and action at a second meeting are curriculum adoptions, school attendance boundary changes, closure of a school site, or addition of a new program. Having several viewpoints present at planning meetings helps ensure that those agenda items needing a full discussion will be presented twice: once for consideration and once again for action.

Those attending the planning session help each other. They consider what information is necessary for the board to make a decision and include the arguments for and against an issue.

The superintendent creates an expectation of critical inquiry to ensure a climate where questions are not just tolerated, but expected. Critical friends are your best friends in agenda planning. This meeting is no place for "yes" persons. Therefore, the superintendent expects the discussion to include potential land mines, which may prevent an even bigger land mine occurring at the meeting. What are the issues likely to bring out opposition and what is the nature of that opposition? Will proactive action by the district head this off through education? Or does the team simply need to be prepared with counterpoints to the opposition?

The planning group thinks strategically regarding the overall direction of the district and how each meeting advances the long-term goals. The group's discussion acts as a mini-rehearsal of the meeting to come. And, importantly, the group is a quality-control body looking for readability and for accuracy. An error-free, jargon-free, clear agenda is ultimately the superintendent's responsibility, but the planning team plays an important role of being the first line of quality control.

THE OVERALL AGENDA

The work of the superintendent and the planning group in developing the agenda for each meeting is, as we have said, akin to that of a secondary teacher developing the master lesson plan for a week. The regular board meeting agenda, like all agendas, has specific content and is used by several audiences. So, like teachers who develop weekly lesson plans, we encourage you to think of the board agenda as a lesson plan. Be clear about objectives (staying mission focused), strategies to achieve the objectives, and ways you will know whether the objectives have been accomplished. (Please see Resource C, p. 153.)

Content

Each meeting's agenda is a combination of critical, high-impact issues and routine items. The 12-month calendar is the starting point because it lists the high-priority and less frequent topics as well as any planned presentations and/or recognitions. Other agenda items are those carried over from the previous meeting, new topics or issues that have arisen and are time sensitive, and the routine items necessary to carry on the district's business. Remember, the board meeting is mission-critical work, so you will want to be sure that all of the topics and discussions are connected to teaching and learning.

Appearance

Chapter 5 provides details about the look of the overall board packet; this is a discussion about the agenda itself and the summary of what is contained in detail in the subsequent material. In some states, laws regulate what must be included on the agenda; in general, however, we recommend that items on the agenda respect the governance role of the board and advance the district's teaching and learning mission.

Any person ought to be able to pick up and scan through the agenda to gain a sense of what issues will come before the board, what action the board is asked to take, and where to find additional information. The title or topic is often insufficient information, so some superintendents include a brief description of the issue, while others use the exact wording of the recommendation the board is being asked to take.

Someone reading over the agenda will want to know for each item whether the board is going to hear a report of information, discuss a topic, or potentially take action on the item. For those items of interest, the person will want to find the item in the board packet along with any additional information provided by supporting documents.

One effective practice for listing agenda items is to group them by major divisions of the district, e.g., issues relating specifically to teaching and learning go under one heading. Districts use a variety of terms for this area such as Curriculum and Instruction, or Educational Services, or Learning Support Services. Other sections could be Human Resources or Personnel; Budget and Finance; and Business Services.

A second method of organizing is by process. Items are broken into the categories of information (little discussion required or expected), discussion, and action. Routine action items are consolidated into one motion. Those that are mission-critical, controversial, or have policy implications are listed as separate action items. Whatever method is chosen, grouping items makes it easier for people to follow the agenda and find their area of interest.

Some superintendents keep the sections in the same order for every meeting, believing the consistency serves the board and readers best. Others like to rotate the sections so all areas receive equal weight, and those at the bottom of the agenda are not always hurried through as the meeting runs late and people become tired.

Timelines

Start with the meeting date and then determine by when the materials must be in the board members' hands. Districts have policies or practices about how far in advance of the meeting the board members must receive the board meeting materials. Some are as few as three days, others are a week. Be sure to allow board members sufficient time to review the material and ask the superintendent any clarifying questions. From that date, work back to the planning meeting and to when you as superintendent must see and approve the items, allowing time to send any item back for revisions if necessary. With all these dates factored in, staff members can develop their own timeline, working back from when they must have their work completed.

We think the best practice is to get materials to the board as far in advance as possible. It takes time to read and think about agenda packets.

If board members are not given sufficient time to read and think critically about the agenda items, the problems become yours! You want board members to have time to read and then question you about anything they may not understand. You do not want these questions coming up for the first time at a board meeting. Remember the "no surprises" rule? Time for all parties to prepare is essential for avoiding surprises.

Audiences

The board meeting is the board doing its work in public. However, although there are opportunities for public input, the meeting is not a public forum; the board has serious business to conduct. If a town hall type meeting is needed, schedule one.

Having said that, we know there are multiple audiences for whom the agenda is important. The board of trustees certainly is the primary one, but there are others, including the district staff, parents, the general public, and the media. Any of these audiences should be able to understand what business is coming before the board by scanning the agenda. Certain items may pique the interest of a parent or member of the public or media. From the agenda, any of these audiences may decide to attend the meeting and perhaps address the board. Members of the media may decide to do a story prior to a board meeting, and this may increase public interest in the item and in the meeting.

A well-prepared agenda communicates effectively to various audiences and can create feedback that is useful to the superintendent in preparing for the meeting itself. Media and general public interest in a particular agenda item alerts superintendents to an issue, and they in turn can prepare the board, attempting to avoid surprises.

INDIVIDUAL AGENDA ITEMS

Earlier we described what the overall agenda looks like, how the agenda is organized, and a typical order in which sections of the agenda appear. However, an effective board meeting is the result of both the general organization and content of the agenda and the attention you pay to the details of each agenda item, report, presentation, and recognition. The meeting is the sum of the parts and each part contributes to or detracts from the whole.

The development of all agenda items requires care. Whether routine and typical district business, one-time topics, or hot and controversial issues, the person preparing the items needs to approach the task with the mind of a teacher creating an informative, high-quality lesson. Sloppy work creates problems no one needs or deserves. We have seen a problem arise in board meetings when a negative response to an insignificant agenda item created a general negativity that carried over to larger, more significant issues.

Here are some questions to consider: What is the agenda format? Who prepares each item? What are the timelines for preparation and submission? Who reviews and approves the items? How do we handle presentations and recognitions?

Deadlines for creating the agenda are critical and include several steps: initial preparation, review by one or more persons, and submission for printing. Respecting the people and tasks of others in the organization, especially the person charged with putting the packet together, begins with adherence to timelines.

Format

As usual, many of our ideas about agendas and board meetings come from our colleagues. They can help us work on our work and make it better.

We know an experienced group of superintendents who brought their agendas to their monthly breakfast meeting. Each of them, from the one with just a year of experience to the veteran of 15 years, walked away with an idea about how to improve agendas or agenda items. It was not that one method of organizing the agenda was right—or even better—than others, just that a new way of organizing had the potential to improve their practice, solve a problem, and make the board meeting flow more smoothly.

From this experience and others, we learned that the overall format for agenda items should be standard, that is, consistent from meeting to meeting. That does not mean never to change it, but rather to think carefully before making a change. You want to be sure the board's energy is on the issues, not navigating through the agenda.

Ensuring full information is the most important thing, for you are asking the board to make decisions critical to student learning and district progress. No decision is any better than the information provided.

The format typically includes the subject/topic line, name of the preparing department or division, background information—what led to the item being presented—a summary of the issue with succinct details, the fiscal impact, and the superintendent's recommendation for board action. Where appropriate, the report also includes options and alternatives, or statements of the pros and cons, and implications and ramifications of the options.

For districts with a strategic, long-range plan and/or a series of goals, it is effective to write the applicable goal on the agenda item. Seeing the goal reminds the staff, as well as the board and public, that the district is working toward the accomplishment of its established goals. This is especially useful when there is an impact on the budget—board members can see how the expenditure of funds is tied to the strategic plan.

The superintendent alone, or in conjunction with the planning group, makes a decision about what to recommend the board do with each agenda item. Considerations include whether to request action or present the item for information and discussion, indicating that certain items will return at a subsequent meeting for action. The other decision is whether to have the action item handled as part of the consolidated motion or individually.

While opinions differ, most superintendents believe they should write their recommendation for board action on the agenda item. You may not want to put a recommendation on a first reading when a topic is for discussion only. However, we believe on all other items it is important for the board to know what their superintendent, their chief educational officer, recommends as the best course of action. Regardless of format, the superintendent needs to know the purpose of the item and how it contributes to the work of the district. Even if a recommendation is not made formally, the superintendent must understand the context of the item and the intended outcomes and unintended consequences that would follow board action.

Two cautions: First, the board, as a governance body, should act on the perceived merits of the item. The board's credibility will be better if it is viewed as a thoughtful body weighing the pros and cons, considering the available information, and reviewing the superintendent's recommendation.

Second, on items with major policy implications, the superintendent may want to defer a formal recommendation until the viewpoints of all parties, including board members, have been heard. That shows a willingness on the part of the superintendent to be a good listener as well as a good leader. A quick decision made in hopes that the situation will be settled happily, or go away, is just not realistic in today's complex political environment.

Writing the proposed action in the form of a motion is helpful to board members, as they can read exactly what the superintendent is recommending. The board member who is "moving" the item can read the recommendation as written or easily modify the words in making the motion. Where the motion is not stated, we have observed board members struggle to create motions, and their uncertainty makes them uncomfortable and often embarrassed. A poorly worded motion can lead to confusion when you and staff try to follow up after the meeting.

One situation we expect will be more common in our multicultural school districts is having a school board member for whom English is his or her second language. We observed a board member struggling to understand all of the issues and having trouble explaining his thoughts clearly in the meeting. As a result, the superintendent arranged for an interpreter to sit next to the board member for assistance, allowing full participation and making him a more productive member of the governing team—and thereby making the team more effective.

A consistent, straightforward agenda format enhances communication. Regardless of the exact format and order, common elements are important: a neat, clean appearance; readable font size; and straightforward, reader-friendly language, with no mistakes. (Proofread, proofread, proofread!)

Originators

Unless the superintendent is the only administrator in the district, other key staff will write agenda items depending on their area of expertise and responsibility. A planning worksheet is one tool for tracking who writes what item. For example, in one district, the cabinet is defined as the assistant superintendents. The cabinet members submit all proposed agenda items on a standard planning sheet to the superintendent's office at least two weeks prior to the next board meeting. The planning group uses the worksheets in their meeting and to track that all items are completed, sent to the superintendent for approval, and finalized for the agenda.

At times, someone other than a cabinet member, such as the director of a grant program, is the one with the expertise and therefore the responsibility to prepare a specific agenda item. In larger districts, this may happen frequently. The person with the expertise drafts the agenda item and submits it to the appropriate division head. The division head can present the item at the planning meeting or invite the originating staff member to attend the planning meeting, especially if the item is deemed potentially controversial.

Review and Approval

Smaller districts have fewer originators and levels of review, if any. In very small districts, the entire responsibility for writing agenda items falls solely on the shoulders of the superintendent and the administrative assistant.

The superintendent must review and approve agenda items, unless it is a very large district where the responsibility may be shared or partially delegated to a deputy. Even in large districts, we think it is important for the superintendent's stamp of approval to be on the completed items and packet. Remember the superintendent who delegated and did not review the agenda? Ultimately, regardless of who wrote the item or reviewed it, the board packet is the superintendent's work product, and therefore, your responsibility. The bottom line, as your mathematics teacher told you, is "Check your work before you turn it in!"

POTENTIAL BOARD ACTION

As indicated earlier, agendas can be organized either by process or district divisions. Regardless of which option the superintendent chooses, we recommend that what the board is expected to do be clearly noted alongside each agenda item. Is the item presented for information only, with little discussion expected? Is it presented for discussion? Is it presented for action?

In most cases, state laws and local board policies provide rules or guidelines as to whether a particular item may be listed as information, discussion, or action, including those items that may be placed on a consent agenda. California, for example, does not allow the board to take action on any item unless it is listed for action. That is, the board cannot discuss a topic listed for information and then decide they are ready to act; rather, the superintendent must post it on a subsequent agenda for action.

Some states have regulations permitting emergency action. Some have laws that require public hearings, or at least some discussion, before an action is taken on particular types of items. Because these rules vary by state, we recommend superintendents check the laws carefully and get advice from legal counsel when necessary.

Information/Discussion Items

Agenda items that are presented for information only sometimes engender considerable board discussion and community input. We believe there is a place for these items whose sole purpose is to educate the board, staff, and community on a matter of educational importance.

Information items are intended to make the board and public aware of a new state policy, actions taken on a request for information by a board member or the entire board (some district policies require a majority of the board to ask for a report), or an update on an existing district or school program. For example, a district may have a practice of hearing a report from each school or department over the course of the year. Information items offer opportunities to inform a variety of audiences on mission-critical activities occurring throughout the district.

Action Items

While most action items are routine in the sense that they appear on every agenda (e.g., purchase orders, personnel assignments, etc.), there are always agenda items that require discussion and deliberation. We think superintendents and boards get themselves in trouble when they try to take action too quickly. Hence the importance of the "two-meeting rule."

"Two-meeting rule" items are those that have major ramifications for students, such as a program called for in the district strategic plan, a change in graduation requirements, school attendance boundaries, or the adoption of a new textbook. Such items require at least two meetings to fully discuss them and decide on appropriate action. Even though it is called the "two-meeting rule," some items because of their complexity or political implications may be on more than two meeting agendas.

Typically, the agenda item is listed for information and discussion only at the first meeting. At that meeting, the public provides input and the board discusses the item. After the board meeting, the superintendent and staff make appropriate changes and prepare the item for action on the next, or a subsequent meeting.

Most discussion items need a simple majority vote of the board. However, some state laws specify a super-majority for certain items. A few other topics require a roll-call vote of the board. Be sure exceptions to a simple majority voice vote are noted on the agenda. This helps the entire board, particularly the board president, to run the meeting effectively.

Not every non-routine item needs two meetings; many can be presented and acted on in one meeting. Approval of a grant application, a construction change order, or approval of a new high school course are possible examples. And, of course, any routine item can become a political hot button requiring more discussion and a delay in action.

Consent Agenda

As described, most agenda items are routine; that is, they reoccur regularly. Examples are purchase orders, pay warrants, recommendations for hiring, acceptance of financial reports, and minutes of regular and special board meetings.

Many districts use a "consent agenda." Items listed under the consent agenda are passed in a single motion, a consolidated motion voted on by the board without discussion. By eliminating the need to vote on each item, the board saves time for the rest of the agenda. Sometimes it is the superintendent's sole responsibility to decide what goes on the consent agenda; other times it is the superintendent and board president; and still other times the superintendent decides in conjunction with the planning group, which may or may not have board members involved.

Whatever the case, be sure to give careful thought to the placement of an item on the consent calendar. It is an especially good idea for the superintendent to review with the board president prior to the meeting which items are appropriate for the consent agenda. Another good strategy is to ask the board at the conclusion of a discussion item whether the item is ready for action as a separate or consent agenda item.

However, as is true for any item on the agenda, any member of the board or the public has the option of "pulling" an item off the consent agenda and asking for individual consideration, questions and answers, and action. If this happens, the item is pulled and is voted on later when it appears on the agenda.

One problem with a consent agenda may be the procedure for a board member to "pull" an item from the consent agenda. The superintendent may suggest that board members who have questions about items on the consent agenda call him or her prior to the meeting for clarification. At one board meeting, we observed some members of the board pulling a number of consent items as a way to give the audience the impression that they were more alert than the other members. A way to counteract this is by having a protocol that all board members adopt—an agreement to call for information about these routine matters prior to the meeting, which will save time and energy and build trust.

The board has a full range of choices, from having no consent agenda to putting the entire agenda on consent. We saw the latter work effectively in one district whose meetings had been unduly long and spent on hashing over the mundane. Requiring board members to pull items from the consent agenda if they wanted further discussion made them aware of focusing on essential topics. The board determined that this approach helped make their meetings, their work as a board, more effective.

The consent agenda can be one general list of items, or it can be arranged as a list of items by department or division such as human resources/ personnel, business and finance, etc. We suggest having the purpose and process of the consent agenda written on the board agenda and on a "Welcome to the Board Meeting" sheet or brochure available at every meeting. Board meetings can be intimidating, especially for those attending a meeting for the first time. Having the rules and procedures in writing reduces the mystery and lets people know how they can participate in the meeting.

In addition to having the consent agenda process written on the agenda and "welcome to the meeting" brochure, it is helpful for the board president to read the purpose and process out loud at the beginning of the meeting and prior to the board taking action. This provides another opportunity to educate the public and ensure everyone's right to participate.

PRESENTATIONS AND RECOGNITIONS

Boards recognize specific students or student groups for their success in academics, athletics, or activities. They laud staff for honors and awards they receive or ways they help their students learn. Others the board thanks are individuals and groups in the community who give their time or money to help students and staff.

Recognitions and performances are positive. However, superintendents must plan these and guide the board as carefully as they do with other agenda items. You need a plan for who or what will be brought into the spotlight and when. Random recognition or poorly planned and executed mini-ceremonies or performances can lead to hurt feelings and even cynicism.

Consider the subtleties. A board that recognizes only winning athletic teams, or repeatedly honors teachers from the highest achieving, highest socioeconomic school, sends a message about what and who is important and what and who is not. The board meeting is full of symbolism, and the message the superintendent wants to send to the community is crafted to fit the style, substance, and goals of the district.

Effective recognition programs are equitable across the district. Staff members pay attention to who is honored and what programs are highlighted, and are quick to point out if one school in one part of town gets most of the notice, or if another is consistently overlooked. To honor and recognize people, programs, and events effectively and fairly, think of a system that over time recognizes staff, students, or volunteers from each school and each grade level or subject area. Remember to include support departments and support staff as well as teaching and administrative staff.

Awards range from the simple, such as a paper certificate, to something more elaborate, perhaps a crystal paperweight. If awards are physical—e.g., Golden Apples for the outstanding employees of the year—they need to be the same for support, administrative, and teaching staff. Again, the subtle message is that every person's contribution is equally valued. Overtly, the superintendent and/or board president can state how each of these people being honored is doing mission-critical work. In addition to equity, the tokens of appreciation should all be of high quality.

An essential part of planning is for the superintendent to make sure honorees are notified of the award or recognition and the date and time of the event so they and their friends and family may attend if they so choose. We have seen meetings where honorees did not appear, and later investigation revealed they were never asked to attend. The same is true for student presentations or performances. The superintendent makes sure the presentations are planned carefully so they are appropriate, dignified, and have the intended effect of acknowledging a job well done with a presentation that is well done.

When the board president or members are going to make comments, present awards, or introduce a performance, the superintendent should help prepare them by having information written out so the facts are accurate, names are pronounced correctly, and the presentation is professionally done. In preparing for student presentations or performances, the superintendent should make sure the adult in charge of the students or groups is aware of the time limits and that those performing have practiced the performances within those limits. It helps, too, to have the adults remind groups of students to act respectfully at all times because the audience and board watch them prior to, as well as during, their performance or recognition.

If staff members are making presentations, you want to make sure they know the time limits. We watched one superintendent glaring at a staff member who was going on and on, and then not so subtly drawing his index finger across his neck in a "cut it off" gesture. Later he admitted he should have given the staff member a time limit. To a staff member passionate about a topic, brief may mean 20 minutes—way longer than for the superintendent who defines brief as 5 minutes.

Some districts have a policy that written reports included with the agenda are not repeated orally. Boards in other districts may decide that a brief oral overview may be useful to the discussion. Most importantly, oral reports by staff need to be an executive summary, that is, concise—as defined by the superintendent.

OTHER MEETING AGENDAS

Not all issues need to be handled in a regular board meeting. Some topics can be addressed through telephone calls, emails, and separate reports to the board. Boards and superintendents also need to be vigilant regarding what is interesting versus what is important, and spend their time on the most important items and in the most effective manner.

But a number of "bigger" topics warrant additional consideration beyond a regular meeting of the board. Some issues might call for a special meeting, town hall or open forum, study session, or workshop. A topic might require in-depth study on an issue, or a work session on a general area of curriculum and instruction or the budget, or additional opportunity for community input, or a workshop for the board's professional development. Each of these meetings requires an agenda and public posting of the meeting, including a time for the public to address the board.

Most special meetings are for information and discussion and not for action. Unless the agenda specifies that action could be taken, the board cannot act. However, as a result of the meeting, the superintendent may prepare an action item for a regular meeting.

Unless the superintendent schedules a special closed-session meeting, these other kinds of meetings are "open," meaning members of the public are notified of the meeting date, time, and location, and are invited to attend. The only meetings of the board not open to the public are specified by each state's laws and involve very limited topics (see Chapter 8).

Special Meeting

The superintendent and board may call a special meeting to discuss one specific, important topic, such as high school graduation requirements. A topic like this one requires more time than is feasible to devote at a regular board meeting. Other examples of special-meeting topics are revisions to a set of board policies, institution of a new curricular program, or acquisition of land for a new school.

Another purpose for a special meeting might be to handle a "hot" item—an issue that has surfaced and demands the board's immediate attention. An example of this occurred when the California state legislature decided to reduce class sizes in Kindergarten through Grade 3. The legislature acted on the first of July and expected school districts to implement the decision when school opened that fall—just two months away—offering financial incentives to do so. In an effort to respond quickly, most California superintendents and school boards were hustling to schedule special meetings and make changes to be ready for the opening of school.

A special meeting is generally for information and discussion only. Or the discussion item may be acted upon at that special meeting or in a follow-up regular meeting. The posted agenda makes it clear what the board will be doing.

Another reason for holding special meetings might be for a joint meeting with another governmental agency. Some boards meet with their local city council, the boards of neighboring school districts, or with other governmental agencies for the purpose of collaborating on projects.

Open Forum or Town Hall

At times the board may want to hold an open forum—a type of town hall meeting during which the board will not take action—if the interest is high in a specific topic or in the district in general. Sometimes the board wants to hear more from the public, for example on a proposed strategic plan or school facilities plan.

Other times there is a hot issue and the public is demanding to have additional input. This happened in one district when the board declared an interest in closing a street between an elementary school and middle school for safer passage of students. Even though this seemed relatively innocuous, residents became incensed because they feared emergency vehicles could not get to their homes using what they saw as the shortest route. The district found it useful to hold two open forums to hear from the residents and the emergency agencies.

If the purpose is to listen—to gain information and hear various viewpoints—then it is important for the board, superintendent, and staff to do just that—listen.

Study Session

A study session can be similar to a special meeting, except at a study session there often is more interaction with staff than at a regular meeting. In fact, it is often helpful to change the seating pattern to encourage more interaction. We also think a study session by its nature should be a deliberative process. Make it clear that the board will not take action. An example is dealing with the budget in good times or bad. Typically, the staff presents information and possible scenarios; the board analyzes the possibilities and asks questions to clarify potential impacts. This give and take is important as the superintendent and staff prepare the budget for adoption. An examination of student assessment data is another topic that lends itself to extensive presentation and discussion.

Other topics appropriate for a study session are student achievement goals, or a potential change in student population, either growth or declining enrollment. Boards must be given available data and helped to understand what they mean in order to set achievement targets.

Enrollment numbers are critical for every district. Whether enrollment is going up or down, the district faces many issues, and board members will want a great deal of information and a high degree of give and take between the board, superintendent, staff, and perhaps special consultants.

As is the case at all meetings of the board, the public is invited and can give input and possibly join in the dialogue; whatever the public's role beyond the usual public comment time should be spelled out in the agenda and reiterated orally by the board president.

Board Workshop

Effective board–superintendent governance teams place a high priority on their own professional growth and development. As pointed out in Chapter 2, an important area of professionalism is a clear understanding of the roles and responsibilities of the boards, individual members, and the superintendent. This topic should be revisited regularly, and always when there is a new board member and/or superintendent. The most effective way to do this is at a board workshop or retreat.

Around the country, many state school boards associations provide training in board governance. Other states hold an annual school boards conference, and of course many school board members choose to attend the annual national school boards conference. But within the school district, a board and a superintendent seeking to improve their individual and collective leadership performance will commit to regular workshops for their own governance team. Not only do these people improve their knowledge, they also model continuous learning for the rest of the staff and the community.

Preparation of the agenda of each type of meeting and the agenda packet are indeed time-consuming and complex processes requiring thoughtfulness. As we have seen, there are many matters and issues to consider. Believe us, the time spent is worthwhile. In fact, we would go so far as to say that the quality of the meeting itself is 90 percent dependent on the quality of the preparation. Doing this job well has a high payoff. However, because we are mindful of that old saying about "the best laid plans of mice and men," we think there are a number of special details in planning the logistics of the meeting itself that deserve some further attention. We turn our attention to those details next.

4

Preparing

Sweat the Small Stuff

"Ben, you own the company. If there's something you don't like about the way business is done, why don't you just do it different?" That had never occurred to me before.

(Cohen & Greenfield, 1997, p. 23)

Most of us have been told at one time or another not to "sweat the small stuff." Good preparation for the board meeting includes what might be viewed as "small stuff." But in this case it's probably a good idea to sweat it—just a bit. The fact is that pre-meeting planning requires careful thought and a conscious decision about how to handle each detail. By paying attention to meeting logistics, we contribute to the effectiveness of the school board meeting. Conversely, ignoring or overlooking logistical details over which we have control will result in a meeting that is less than effective, and in some cases counterproductive.

Take the example of legendary coach John Wooden (1997) instructing his UCLA basketball players in agonizing detail including, much to their impatience, how to put their socks on properly. He insisted every player practice this over and over again. How to put on one's socks may seem like a minor detail considering the multitude of skills and plays a college team needs to learn. But Coach Wooden knew that if a player got a blister because his sock was rubbing, his ability to play and to focus his full attention on the game would be inhibited.

He is right; his logic and wisdom are unimpeachable. Attention to detail improves the chance of success. After all, it is pretty difficult to run hard and turn quickly with a bad blister.

While we do not include "putting on socks" as part of our board meeting preparation ideas, we do suggest that Wooden's words about putting on socks "with careful attention," have implications for our work. When superintendents pay attention to details within their control, they are likely to produce a much better board meeting.

As you consider different options for handling the logistics of a meeting, it is probably good to remember there are no absolute rights or wrongs. There are, however, advantages and disadvantages to each option. Therefore, we believe it is important to take the time to consider which options make the most sense for your individual district and which help the district focus on its teaching and learning mission.

We are also mindful that many existing practices are there for a reason and even may be part of a long-standing tradition. Be sure you know the reason before making a change, especially if you are a new superintendent. Change for improvement is sound practice; change for change's sake is not. This may seem obvious, but we have seen superintendents who think they have to make their mark by quick, decisive (read "impulsive") moves that unnecessarily tamper with an important tradition. The result is usually an initial erosion of the confidence the board has in the superintendent's work.

Consequently, we urge superintendents to make their mark by thoughtful change that leads to improvement. In most instances, it makes little difference how good a change may be if it results in a battle. Spending the time to achieve "buy-in" is generally well worth any delay in instituting a change.

So, what are these details that influence the quality of a meeting before it starts? They tend to fall into three areas: general meeting logistics such as time and place; details of the meeting room itself; and considerations for the people who attend the meeting. And let's not forget a fourth, a concern that lurks in the mind of every superintendent: What might come up at the meeting that we did not expect? How does one prepare for the unexpected?

GENERAL LOGISTICS

General logistics include meeting details such as location, frequency, day of the week, time of the day, and the ending time. Televising meetings brings its own set of issues, each needing thoughtful analysis, as televising can be an asset or a nightmare—and sometimes both.

Location

Should the meeting always be in the same location? What are the pluses and minuses of holding all meetings in the same location versus holding meetings in various locations throughout the school district? Can you or should you televise meetings, and if so, how does that affect the choice of location?

Using the Same Location

Many districts have a Board Meeting Room designed to accommodate the maximum number of people at a typical meeting. For a district without a boardroom, sometimes a classroom, library, or cafeteria is used.

Using the same location for every board meeting, even if the room is not specifically designated as the board meeting room, is often the simplest and most cost-effective option. It is the option we recommend. The same person or crew can set up the room each time, using the same materials and equipment that are kept in the room or nearby. Using the same room for meetings means little time and/or attention is needed to assure details are in place and not forgotten; the logistics do not tend to vary, but rather are routine and predictable.

Even with a standard location, a "hot" issue may cause the superintendent to move a meeting to a larger location where more people can attend. We encourage you to think ahead and have a plan in place for the time when an unusual or controversial issue arises, just as a teacher has a plan for relocating his or her class for a special program, such as a play the students are performing for parents.

Count on the frustration or anger level rising among both board members and the public when a meeting room location is too small to hold the crowd. Other points of contention are when visitors cannot find the location, or if they find it, cannot locate a place to park. If you change the location of the meeting to accommodate a larger-than-normal crowd, be absolutely certain to publicize the new location and time well ahead of the meeting, complete with detailed directions and a map.

A key person is the one who is asked to manage the clerical and logistical tasks of the board meeting. Whether the meetings are held at the traditional site or at various sites, this staff person double checks the sound system, has nametags at the right spots, and attends to a myriad of small details that contribute to the effectiveness of the whole. In many smaller districts this could be you. Whoever it is, treat this person with respect.

The critical issue is to reduce every potential point of contention you can so the topic can be addressed without additional, avoidable frustrations. Preplanning these details will lower—not eliminate—irritants, and will moderate negative responses and increase the likelihood of turning attitudes to the positive.

Rotating Among Schools

Some boards like to rotate the meetings among some or all of the schools in the district. What are the pros and cons of rotation? Some boards believe more parents and community members will attend meetings if they are held at the schools. In addition, some feel it is a way for board members to be out in the schools. Being out in the schools is important for board members, both to see and be seen by teachers and students. The question is whether holding a school board meeting at individual schools is effective in achieving that goal.

Parent participation may or may not increase with a change of venue. It is a good idea to prepare board members for the reality that attendance may not increase so they are not disappointed if they choose to rotate meetings among various schools.

Take the example of a board that had met in a standard location and decided to go to four different schools over a four-month period. Despite each principal's special efforts to get the parents to the meeting at their school, attendance was very low. In fact, the board received some negative comments from meeting "regulars" that the board was moving the meetings around to make it harder on them and any critics who monitor the board.

One option is to have meetings at special sites for special purposes. Consider holding a board meeting in a newly built or recently refurbished school. Invite parents and community members to participate in student-led tours prior to the meeting. Even if the visitors do not stay for the meeting, they have seen the result of the board and staff's work—and that of their tax dollars.

Another option is to feature a school at a regular board meeting. This could be in the form of a presentation or performance. We particularly like the idea of using the board meeting as an opportunity for the school leadership team to review the progress it is making toward student-related achievement goals.

If the board wants to begin rotating board meetings among sites, you will want to take a number of steps. Most important is to ensure the location is clearly communicated and advertised well in advance of the meeting in the local newspaper, school newsletters, and on the Web site, if applicable. Even with advanced notification, it is a good idea to put a sign on the door of the regular meeting room with the date and time of the current meeting and a map to the location.

Using Other Public Facilities

Sharing facilities with other governmental agencies, such as using City Council Chambers, thus sparing the expense of creating the district's own public meeting room, is another option that may be open to superintendents and boards. Such sharing can also be symbolic, demonstrating a spirit of cooperation. An example of such an instance is a school district and city working together to acquire land and building a joint facility that served each of their needs. This project required a number of joint meetings and resulted in a successful collaboration.

Televising Meetings

Some districts have a well-established practice of televising meetings. There are also many districts where it is neither practical nor desirable to televise meetings. For districts that are thinking about televising meetings, there are multiple factors to consider. Cost is one; location another. Portable video cameras in school cafeterias just do not work effectively enough to capture the content and tone of a meeting.

Televising meetings adds subtle issues for the board and superintendent to discuss. Since most board members are novices at being "on camera," you may need to discuss with them how being on television influences and magnifies behavior. A problem we have seen repeatedly is when one board member comments on an item and then all the other members feel the need to do so, extending meetings far beyond what is necessary. You may need to remind your board members—and have them discuss this—that despite having a viewing audience, it is still a meeting of the board to do the district's business, not a forum for talking to the people in their homes. It might also be good to mention to board members that they may never know when they are on camera, and there are no retakes. Think about what television was like in the 1940s and '50s when everything was shot live. Avoid those potentially embarrassing moments!

Today's viewers are used to quality video and television productions, so it is essential to have skilled technical staff. Viewers have little tolerance for amateurish productions like the one we once viewed (an extreme example, we admit) where a soap dispenser on the wall appeared to be sitting on a board member's head.

Choosing an Option

If meetings are televised, the options for the location may be restricted. Nevertheless, within whatever latitude you have, make decisions about the most effective arrangements to meet specific goals, weighed against the reality of the costs, both financial and human.

Base the decision about where you hold board meetings on the pros and cons of each available option. Does having the meeting at the same time and place, on the same day of the week, reduce confusion for the public and staff? Has the cost of custodial time been figured into the budget for the meeting?

A meeting held at a school site will take the principal's time to work with the superintendent's office to make sure everything that is likely to be needed is ready. Each time a different school is involved, it is a first-time experience for the principal and custodian, requiring coordination from all the participants. These include the superintendent or designee, the superintendent's assistant, and possibly other district staff who need to move furniture. Setup and tear down require people and time. On the plus side, many principals like the opportunity to showcase their school and their students' work.

Frequency

How frequently a board meets may be a matter of habit rather than necessity. Effective superintendents will ask themselves and their boards these questions: Are we meeting too often to be effective in making decisions and carrying out the work? Are our scheduled meetings too far apart and slowing our progress?

How you answer these questions and the decisions you make regarding the frequency of your meetings have a critical impact on the entire organization. Every board meeting requires significant superintendent and staff time to plan, prepare, attend, and follow up after the meeting. Each meeting requires commitment of time and effort of all board members. This time commitment must be balanced with time necessary for staff to carry out the rest of their responsibilities, to attend to the daily and weekly maintenance tasks required to run a complex organization—tasks that are essential to achieving the goals the board has set for the district.

Among the many options are these: meeting once a month; meeting twice a month; meeting twice some months and once in other months such as December, a spring month where there are extended holidays, or in the summer, particularly for districts on a traditional rather than a year-round calendar. When two meetings per month is the norm, some districts find it effective to alternate the content of meetings, attending to all of the business items at one meeting and devoting the next meeting to curriculum and instruction topics. This degree of purity between the two agendas is not always possible. However, having every other meeting focus on instruction sends a powerful message that teaching and learning deserve and receive the attention of the board.

Our recommendation because of the time and expense involved is to hold the fewest meetings necessary to do the important business of the district. Time spent in meetings for the sake of meeting takes time away from other work the staff could be doing, and other events board members could attend. The effective board governs rather than manages. Remember, all boards have the option of holding additional meetings, or study sessions or workshops, when issues warrant. The board also can cancel meetings if there is no need to meet, or if items can be held for a future meeting.

Day and Time

Tradition and convenience are typical reasons why board meetings are held on a certain day of the week, start at a specific time of day, and end at a set time. The timing of closed meetings is also often a result of tradition and habit. Closed meetings can be held before, during, or after open sessions.

Because circumstances, including the composition of the board and superintendent team, change over time, it is useful to examine periodically the current practice and determine if it continues to be the most effective for reaching desired outcomes. In addition to reviewing the day of the week and meeting starting time, it is helpful to look at having a set ending time, as well as to determine the most effective time to conduct closed sessions.

Day of the Week

Districts assess the optimum day of the week to hold a meeting based on board members' schedules, district activities, other community meetings, and staff time needed to prepare and distribute materials for the board meeting.

Candidates for a board seat may know the current practice and can change their schedules to accommodate the meeting night. However, others may not be able to change their schedule, and so particularly after the election of a new member, the entire governance team must reexamine what day of the week works for everyone.

Superintendent and staff schedules, while not the primary factors, are important to consider. You need to prepare for meetings and follow up after them, and meetings on a certain day of the week may facilitate your work.

Starting Time

What time of day are meetings held? Do they start in the morning, afternoon, or evening? Should all the meetings start at the same time? Considerations for when meetings begin include the board members' schedules, public access to meetings, staff availability, and something we will talk about later, recovery time.

Board members' schedules are the first consideration. If a member who works does not get off work until 5:00 p.m., the meeting should be started at 5:30 or 6:00 to accommodate that member's schedule.

A second consideration is accessibility for the community. What starting time will allow for members of the public to attend the meeting and speak on topics of interest to them? Are the meetings at a time when working parents can attend? Some boards have found a 4:00 p.m. start time is effective and allows for public comment at the beginning and toward the end of the meeting. Those who do not like to be out at night may speak to the board in the late afternoon; those who are busy all afternoon can address the board in the early evening.

Special meetings on specific topics should always take into account the ability of those particularly interested in the topic to attend. For example, let's assume you have scheduled a meeting to discuss second-language acquisition. If the audience will be primarily people who work all day and have small children, it is best to hold the meeting in the evening and find a way to have childcare available. Not only does this accommodate people with small children, it welcomes them.

With the complexity and "busyness" of peoples' lives today, selecting a time that is most accessible for parents and the community is increasingly difficult. If the meeting starts at 5:00 or 6:00 in the evening, it may interfere with dinnertime or sports. If the meeting starts later in the evening, it may interfere with other meetings. There is no way to satisfy every person, but the discussion alone is a signal that the board and superintendent are trying to accommodate public interest.

Ending Time

An effective superintendent discusses the length of board meetings with the board. Some governance teams set an ending time as a way to be more focused and effective with their time. Many have found that long meetings lead to less effective decision making; items at the end of an agenda sometimes do not get the attention they deserve and would be better carried over to the next meeting. You need to be sure, however, not to carry over a time-sensitive item.

An example of an ending-time policy is a board that starts meetings at 7:00 p.m. and sets 10:00 p.m. as its deadline for ending. At 9:30 p.m., the president reviews the remaining agenda items and requests that board members address any time-sensitive items in case they cannot finish the entire agenda. This district's policy is that the meeting can be extended by a vote of a supermajority of the board in increments of 20 minutes.

Another district had a policy of extending the meeting by increments of 15 minutes with a supermajority vote, in their case meaning four of five board members had to approve. The board finds this practice to be effective in moving the meeting expeditiously yet allowing flexibility when the situation warrants.

Closed Session

Boards are allowed by state law to hold executive, or closed sessions, on a few specific topics. Typically, these are held the same day or night of regularly scheduled board meetings.

When is it best to hold closed or executive sessions? Some prefer to hold them prior to the open meeting; others prefer after. As with any choice, there are pros and cons to each alternative.

The governance team may want to try out certain practices related to days and times and then assess their effectiveness. Please see Chapter 8 for options regarding many aspects of conducting closed sessions.

THE MEETING ROOM

The meeting room itself is a player in a board meeting. The room needs to be functional and professional, yet comfortable and welcoming. How the room is set up, how it looks, and how it feels all contribute to the effectiveness of a meeting and should not be left to chance. The wise superintendent looks at each of these factors with a critical eye, knowing outsiders will form their first impressions the minute they walk into the meeting room. We want to note, however, that one superintendent and board deliberately chose to hold some meetings in facilities that needed substantial work as a way of eliciting community support for a school renovation bond issue. So, again, be thoughtful about what you do and why.

Function

The meeting room has to fulfill its intended purpose—being a place where the board conducts its important work. Ideally, the board members and the superintendent sit in the front of the room away from the entrance door, facing the audience.

If anyone—staff, students, parents, community members—will be making a presentation, the required equipment, such as overhead projector, LCD panel, and screen, are ready before the meeting starts. Being ready includes testing all equipment to make sure it works. Burned-out bulbs, cords not long enough to reach outlets, and a screen of inadequate size are all details that can be avoided with planning and rehearsal. Place the screen in a location to allow the board members, staff, and audience to see clearly, ideally without people having to get up and move around.

Other types of meetings, such as an open forum or study session, usually warrant a different room arrangement from the normal school board meeting. A square or rectangular table facilitates the give and take between board members, the superintendent, and staff, or other outside experts.

Comfort

What does the meeting room look like? Is it clean and well maintained? Does it have good lighting? Is the furniture of good quality and yet not extravagant? The room should be professional, yet inviting. An example of a professional-looking room is one that indicates important business will be conducted but is not lavish. The furniture matches, the room is painted and free of dirt and scratch marks, tables are functional workspaces, and lighting is adequate.

Heating and cooling must be regulated for the size of the crowd, and this often means having someone on duty who is ready to make necessary adjustments. This is particularly important when controversial issues are discussed and emotions run high. Hot issues and a hot room are not good partners. Nor do sweaty superintendents addressing hot issues impress visitors to the meeting.

Ambiance

We like to think of ambiance as another opportunity to remind the audience of the vital work of the board and district staff, and the high esteem in which we hold the education of our youth.

Is student work displayed—both artistic and academic? Are the district's logo, mission, values, and goals posted? Are there awards and recognitions displayed? Is there additional information such as brochures about the district, its schools and programs, available to interest and educate a first-time visitor? In a nutshell, room ambiance presents a wonderful opportunity for the board meeting to reflect a focus on powerful teaching and learning throughout the district.

If the practice is to open the meeting with the Pledge of Allegiance, is the American flag in a prominent place so everyone knows where to face when they stand to recite the Pledge? If there is a state and/or distinguished school flag, are they placed in proper relationship to the U.S. flag?

How the room looks and feels contributes to the image of the district. We have been in board meeting rooms where broken furniture was stacked in the back of the room. We have also seen rooms with loose ceiling tiles and rain stains on the walls. Consider that visitors may respond negatively to seeing broken furniture, etc., and may associate these with low standards and a lack of quality education for the students. But if it is there for a reason, note it and say why the problem exists and what will have to be done to fix it.

PARTICIPANTS

People are the heart and soul of a school district—the board and superintendent of course, but also the staff, the parents, the community, and most important, the students. The details of a meeting specifically related to the people attending can enhance or detract from a board meeting. These include where the board, superintendent, staff, and public sit. Arrangements for the participation of each group are important. So are the specific accommodations for the public—how you welcome them, where they are seated, and how they participate. The effective superintendent attends to all of these details.

Board and Superintendent

You will want to give specific thought to where the board president/chair, the other trustees, and superintendent sit. This includes both the physical seating arrangements and the symbolic effect of who is sitting where.

Seating

Seating of the board and superintendent is important to think about both in terms of function and symbolism. For districts with "board meeting rooms," some aspects may be predetermined, unless the board and superintendent decide a change is worth the potential cost for altering the room. Limitations may also occur when the district shares a facility with another organization.

For example, there may be a fixed, elevated dais. Some boards prefer this; others want to be seated at the same level as the audience so they seem less removed and more receptive. If there are no permanent, built-in seating arrangements, the options are broader. In all cases, a horseshoe configuration is preferable to block seating, that is, everyone sitting in a straight row, since the horseshoe allows the governance team to look at each other as they discuss issues and take action as a collective body.

In terms of the governance team—trustees and the superintendent—who sits where matters. Does the superintendent sit next to the board president in the middle or at the end of the governance team, or as another member at one end of the board table? Does the board sit together with the superintendent at a separate table? We believe the superintendent is integral to a team approach to district leadership and must sit next to the board president. This is primarily functional so the superintendent can quietly advise the board president. It is also symbolic, as meeting attendees observe a team approach between the superintendent and the board president and other members.

Where each board member sits also deserves careful attention from the superintendent and the board chair. Personality conflicts and/or alliances between members are a frequent occurrence. Sometimes there is a very difficult, combative board member whose behavior is moderated by being seated next to a particular board member. Obvious factions on the board can affect the board's work and also send a message to the community about whether the board is united in its goals. There are no hard-and-fast rules about where each person sits. It just makes sense for the seating to enhance the positive participation of each board member.

Details to Enhance Participation

Is there a nameplate for each person at the board table? Is the print large enough for members of the audience to identify members and superintendent by name? Are the nameplates matching with the same size type for each person?

This last point may seem silly. But remember John Wooden's attention to detail? We have seen nameplates with different-size printing, which became an issue when certain board members felt less valued. In one instance, a board had standard-size slots where the administrative assistant slid nameplates in and out. Because one board member's name was short, the letters were large; for another member who had a long name, the letters were very small so they would fit in the same space. Clearly there are simple, inexpensive solutions to this. Attention to detail reduces opportunities for disharmony.

Are there pitchers of water on the board table within the members' reach and water glasses at each place? If someone prefers coffee or a soda, are there attractive cups or glasses available? Think about the subtle message sent by having all board members use professional-looking glasses rather than a variety of paper cups or cans of soda. Appearance counts. Providing a "modesty panel," a metal or wood panel that runs the length of the board table in front, can improve the comfort of board members and contribute to a professional look.

Do board members have supplies they might need to take notes—paper, Post-it notes, pens, or pencils? Ask the trustees for their preferences and provide what helps them do their best work. Passing notes at the board table needs to be done sparingly, but a quick note between the superintendent and board president can keep meetings on track with little fuss. Some superintendents occasionally put a small memento, such as a school coffee mug or piece of candy or a pencil with a school mascot and name, at each board member's place prior to the start of the meeting as a thank-you gesture.

Is there a microphone for each board member and the superintendent? Even in a small room, microphones can help the audience hear without straining. Are microphones set up so people can comfortably sit up to talk into them? Speakers who have to lean over and down to talk into microphones look awkward and unprofessional. Again, this is an example where appearance as well as function matters. Finally, a caution: if the microphones are always on, all sounds can be picked up. Superintendents are advised to remind board members of this to prevent embarrassment.

The Staff

Where do the key staff members sit? Depending on the size of the district, key staff includes assistant superintendents and directors and/or principals. Are staff members easily accessible to the superintendent when special information is needed? In some districts, the senior staff sit at the dais with the board and superintendent; in others, they sit at a table in an easy line of sight of the superintendent. Still others have the staff sit in the audience either randomly or in a prescribed location. The best guideline is to decide what arrangement is efficient for the superintendent to make the board meeting the most effective.

Seating of the secretary or administrative assistant to the board and superintendent is critical. The assistant is responsible for taping the meeting and/or taking notes and making certain all actions are recorded accurately. Therefore, the assistant must be able to see and hear the discussion and actions of the board as well as the input of the staff and public. We recommend the assistant sit at one end of the board horseshoe or at a table right near the board president and superintendent.

The Public

While members of the public have a limited active role in board meetings, how they are treated influences their support for district programs and their image of the district. Smart superintendents think about how people are welcomed to the meeting, what materials are available to help them follow the meeting, where they are seated, and how they are to participate in the meeting where appropriate. Remember, the audience member today may be your board member tomorrow.

Welcome

How are members of the public greeted when they come to the meeting? We recommend that you or a senior staff member greet the public as they enter and that you, the staff, or board members say, "Hello and thank you for coming" or "Is there anything I can do for you?"

Welcoming people to the meeting not only sets an open and inclusive tone, it can also alert you and the board to potential special interests. Welcoming members of the media can pay off in the short and long run in developing positive relations. If non-English speakers attend the meetings or there is an agenda item for non-native speakers of English, information needs to be in the appropriate languages with translators available at the meeting whenever possible.

Materials

Do you have printed material regarding the meeting located near the entrance to make it easy for members of the public to find and understand? Is there a "welcome letter" stating the district's appreciation for their attendance and describing what they can expect at the meeting?

In addition to the agenda summary, have copies of the full board packet available. The number can be estimated by typical meeting attendance. When there is a particular issue of interest to the public, you can increase the number of board packets or have extra copies of the item people have come to hear.

Having information about how a member of the public can offer input on items both on and off the agenda is important. Districts use different terms for the form that members of the public must fill out in order to address the board. Typical terms are Request to Speak cards, hold cards, and blue (or yellow, or some other color) cards. We like to use the term Request to Speak cards. This card typically asks speakers to fill in information the district wants, or is required by state law, and the item they wish to address. The card should note to whom the speaker is to hand the card.

A few districts have developed a "Civility Policy." This outlines the expected and desired behavior of the audience as well as of the board and staff. A caveat is always that such a policy can in no way limit authorized free speech, and different states have various opinions on what this means in terms of oral and written speech—and dress. Have copies of such a policy available on the same table as other visitor information.

Seating

The meeting is for the board to do its work, but it is also a public meeting so the community can observe their work in action. Those attending the meeting must be able to see and hear clearly.

How is the public seating arranged? Are the chairs close to or far away from the board? Is the seating comfortable? Are the chairs in good repair, neat and clean? Are there extra chairs close at hand in case a larger audience appears?

Speakers

Is the public speakers' podium positioned so the speaker addresses the board or the audience? Since this is a meeting of the board in public, speakers are there to address the board, not perform for the audience; therefore, we recommend the speaker podium face the board. Is the podium a comfortable distance from the board? Is the microphone easily adjustable and simple to use? Is a staff member prepared to assist the speaker if there is difficulty with the equipment or with the guidelines?

Most people addressing the board are nervous—in fact, many speakers begin their comments by saying they are nervous or have never addressed the board. Preparing logistically for the maximum comfort, and having staff ready to assist, are examples of those details with a positive payoff both in the short and long run. We are a people business and everyone deserves fair and respectful, tactful treatment. Often the extra effort to make critics welcome reduces the level of anger or upset.

THE UNEXPECTED

One thing superintendents expect is the unexpected. Effective superintendents try their best to prepare for any eventuality, knowing they cannot anticipate every possibility. Some board agenda items we know will be controversial. Planning for those is de rigueur. It is the ones that seem benign only to become controversial that cause superintendents anguish.

One superintendent in a very high-achieving district told us he had two rules: 1. Everything is an issue; 2. When you think something is not going to be an issue, see rule number one. Then there are those items brought up at the public comment section that are not on the agenda, such as the speaker who picked up an old football helmet at the dump and wanted to know why the district was discarding valuable equipment.

Few districts have security personnel at every board meeting, although for some very large districts this is standard practice. Since special circumstances warranting security could arise in any district, knowing and assessing your options for assuring safety at board meetings is necessary long before a problem develops. Examples of "hot button" topics are school attendance boundary changes, changing bus stops, and closing a school.

When superintendents believe an issue could become volatile, they have the option of arranging for extra staff to be present. In unusual cases, superintendents may bring in security personnel, either plainclothes or uniformed, to help ensure safety. Non-uniformed staff may lower the anxiety, but there are times when security should be very visible and uniforms are an asset.

If security personnel are brought in, superintendents need to be sure that staff and the officers are given clear direction on expectations for handling issues. Superintendents must weigh the issues of safety and order with the reality that the presence of security officers not only changes the dynamics of the meeting, but also may affect the image of the district.

A board received considerable negative publicity when a board president had an emotional reaction to a speaker who was criticizing a district staff member. The president ordered security to arrest and remove the speaker from the meeting room. You cannot undo an action like that. In all cases, the superintendent will want to work with the board president regarding how to handle difficult situations.

The superintendent must alert all board members of potential controversies, security arrangements, and contingency plans. An example of a contingency plan might be to move the meeting to a different location if a bigger-than-expected audience appears. This is a judgment call.

Sometimes you can move the meeting and other times it would create more difficulty.

If moving is not feasible, the staff can be ready with sound equipment in a nearby room or in the hallway so the overflow crowd can hear. Staff members can be ready to copy additional agendas or agenda items and move among the audience to hand out Request to Speak cards and answer questions.

Be prepared that a person or group bringing an issue to the board or protesting a potential board action may alert the media. Make every effort to accommodate the media as well as possible, but do not let them run the show. Balance the needs of the media with those of the members of the public.

When we consider security, dealing with the unexpected, and the other details that are part of board meeting preparation, it is clear that details do matter. Here's the overriding, critical point: Make a conscious decision about each part of the pre-meeting planning. Preparation, careful consideration, and communication are vital to increasing the opportunity of having an effective meeting. It is often the small details that either lead to, or derail, an effective school board meeting.

5

Designing the Board Packet

During those early months, I wasn't sure how to construct an agenda, nor did I ever think that it could be a creative, interesting, and innovative document.

(Johnston, et al., 2002, p. 51)

Creating a high-quality board packet for a school board meeting that respects the governance role of the board and supports achievement of the district's mission is not a random act. Just as the superintendent and the staff carefully prepare the board meeting agenda and each agenda item, so should they organize the agenda packet to support discussion and actions by displaying information for board, staff, and community on mission-critical decisions facing the board. Viewed through this lens, the board packet becomes an important planning document and valuable communication tool.

As a planning document, the packet contains some agenda items designed to accomplish short-range goals and others to achieve long-range goals. In that sense, the information in the packet supports both essential governance activities as it helps the board, superintendent, and staff to think strategically and plan systematically. Each action becomes a layer upon which the next layer fits, moving the district toward achieving its mission and goals.

The board packet communicates with four main audiences: the board, the staff, parents and community stakeholders, and the media. The primary audience is the board because they use the information the superintendent provides to make decisions. The second audience is the staff. A handful of staff will be directly involved in creating the board packet, but staff members across the district are affected by decisions made by the board. Principals, teachers, and support staff read the board packets to learn what the board is dealing with, monitor what the board is doing, and participate in those areas that interest and affect them.

As the third audience, parents and community members judge the quality of the district based on what they see. They take note of the clarity of presentation of the overall agenda as well as each agenda item. People notice whether the language is straightforward, sensitive, and inclusive. The obvious as well as the subtle influence their opinions about the district and the board and superintendent's leadership.

Members of the media, the fourth audience, scan board packet agendas to see topics of interest to them. They can write a story before the meeting based on the report itself, call for additional information, or attend the meeting. Because many districts now put their board agendas and/or entire board packets on the Web, the media and others are able to access critical information much more quickly. This expands the audience, making attention to detail and quality even more critical. We think designing the packet with these audiences in mind helps the superintendent create a packet that increases each group's ability to see and understand issues.

The superintendent in concert with the board must be sure the design of the meeting packet works for the board. Superintendents have many options in putting together the board packet, each of which can influence the effectiveness of the meeting. As superintendents, you will be taking the lead in evaluating the effectiveness of the packet for accomplishing the board's business, but be cautious and do not change elements of the packet or its design too fast. Also consult with the board president, and then the whole board, as you seek continuous feedback to make improvements.

We found a good example of a superintendent who moved cautiously, but immediately, and involved the board in her efforts to make the board packet more efficient. She was an experienced superintendent who was selected to lead a new district. Prior to beginning her new job, she observed two meetings of the board where she saw board members' apparent frustration as they tried to follow each agenda item in the board packet. They did not lose their tempers, but their anxiety and irritation were obvious.

As soon as she took over the job, this superintendent began designing a board packet that was user-friendly. Equally important, she also developed a plan for how to introduce changes to the board and staff.

Remembering to honor traditions and current practice, she suggested a few simple modifications to the packet, explaining the changes in terms of what she had observed at the board meetings she had attended earlier. Typical statements were, "I was noticing that you had to flip back and forth in the packet on a certain item and was thinking I could make a couple changes in our presentation that might make it more effective for you."

After a couple of meetings, the superintendent asked the board to evaluate how the changes worked for them in terms of easing the logistics and whether they improved their ability to focus on the issues. The board, finding success, was open to further modifications. By moving incrementally and involving the board, the superintendent was able to develop an agenda packet that improved the effectiveness of the board meetings by allowing the board to focus on content, not logistics.

The board packet can take a variety of formats and should be attractive. The overriding point is to organize the packet so it enables board members to do their work effectively. Ask yourself these questions: Does the packet have a consistent, logical flow that allows board members to be confident they have all the information they need? Can they find the information they need in order to make a high-quality decision? In addition, is it clear to members of the public and the staff what business is coming before the board? The "buzz" needs to be about ideas, not about people struggling to find the right page or having to guess what the board is doing.

Areas you will want to think about include the key elements of every board packet, backup or supporting documents, the appearance of the packet, and other details that can make a big difference in the pace and tone of the meeting, which will be discussed in the next section.

KEY ELEMENTS OF THE BOARD PACKET

Board meeting packets tend to have the following components: a cover page, an agenda that serves as a table of contents, and a series of sections, most often one for each of the district's main divisions. Within each section are the agenda items that relate to that division. We will suggest guidelines to be used in planning each of these elements.

Cover Page

Former Scandinavian Airlines CEO Jan Carlzon (1987) believed the company's employees had 15 seconds to win, or lose, a new customer. Here is another example of the importance of first impressions. Through conducting research on thousands of interviews to hire new employees, the fact emerged that many interviewers made up their minds about a person being interviewed for a position in the first 7 seconds, based on the person's appearance.

We know first impressions matter, and that, in fact, you never get another chance to correct a first impression. With this in mind, remember that first-time meeting attendees get their initial impression from the meeting room, how they are welcomed, and the look of the board meeting packet, starting with the cover. Make the cover of the board packet attractive as well as informative. This doesn't mean expensive; it means attractive and reflective of the quality of the district. Typically, the packet cover displays the district name; the district logo; mission statement; and of course, the date, time, and place of the open meeting and the closed-session meeting. Superintendents often find it useful to include the date, time, and location of the next meeting.

Aspects affecting the attractiveness of the cover include the quality of the paper, size of font, clarity of information, and simplicity. Each of these elements contributes to a straightforward, professional, businesslike tone for the board meeting.

Agenda

Like all meeting agendas, this one gives the order of business: call to order; Pledge of Allegiance; roll call of board members; approval of the agenda; presentations and recognitions; public comment; and consolidated motion, action, and discussion items. Whatever order you decide on, the board follows this sequence of events throughout the meeting unless a board member, or you, requests a change of order for a particular reason. The other reason to deviate from the order listed is if there are "time-certain" items when the board will take up a specific item at a specific time.

We recommend when a procedure is not obvious, that a brief explanation be written on the agenda. For example, a new attendee likely will be unfamiliar with the purpose and process of a consent agenda, where the board approves several items in one consolidated motion. Therefore, just after the title Consent Agenda (or Consolidated Motion) and before the list of items, write a brief description and rationale for this action, such as the following:

> The purpose of the Consolidated Motion is to expedite action on routine agenda items. These items will be acted upon with one motion, second, and approval of the board unless a member of the board or public wishes to pull the item for individual discussion and action. If a member of the public wishes to speak to an item on the Consolidated Motion, please complete a "hold card" (Request to Speak) and turn it in to the superintendent's assistant prior to the board taking action.

Another district might write it this way:

> All matters listed under Consent Agenda are those on which the board has previously deliberated or that can be classified as routine items of business. An administrative recommendation on each item is contained in the agenda supplements. There will be no separate discussion of these items prior to the time the Board of Trustees votes on the motion unless members of the board, staff, or public request specific items to be discussed or pulled from the Consent items.

Members of the public also need to know how they should go about addressing the board regarding an item on the agenda or a topic not on the agenda. Having this process in writing on the agenda as well as in the "Welcome to the Board Meeting" letter or brochure invites people to participate. This is particularly important if people are upset; in addition to being concerned about a topic, they will also be frustrated if they cannot figure out the process of speaking to the board.

Here is a typical written instruction to insert:

> **Comments on Agenda Items:** If you wish to speak regarding an item on the agenda, please complete a blue speaker slip located at the sign-in desk and present it to the Secretary to the Board prior to the start of the meeting. When the Board President invites you to the podium, please state your name, address, and organization before making your presentation.

The following are other examples of statements and processes a district might use:

> **Public Comments:** Persons wishing to address the board on any school related issue not listed elsewhere on the agenda are invited to do so under the "Public Comments" item. In the interest of time and order, presentations from the public are limited to three (3) minutes per person and the total time for non-agenda items shall not exceed twenty (20) minutes. An individual speaker's allotted time may not be increased by a donation of time from members of the public in attendance. If you wish to speak under Public Comments, please complete a blue speaker's slip and follow the directions for speaking to agenda items. Complaints or charges against an employee are not permitted in an open meeting of the Board of Trustees.

> In accordance with the xxx Act, unless an item has been placed on the published agenda, there shall be no action taken. The Board may 1) acknowledge receipt of the information, 2) refer to staff for further study, or 3) refer the matter to the next agenda.

As we will point out again in Chapter 10, an effective practice, in addition to having the statement written on the agenda, is for the board president to read this procedure out loud at the beginning of the meeting to ensure that people understand. This also gives them a few minutes to fill out and turn in the Request to Speak card. Patience, especially when dealing with angry people, is a virtue.

Table of Contents—"The Executive Summary"

The table of contents informs the public, staff, and the press of the topics and issues the board is going to consider. A clear, concise table of contents functions as an executive summary. It lists each agenda item, provides a brief (one to four lines) summary of each, and states the superintendent's recommendation in the form of a motion.

Often this summary is the only part of the document the public or staff in the schools and departments read. If so, they should be able to understand from the summary what business is coming before the board. Staff and public often decide on the basis of the summary whether they wish to attend the meeting, hear the discussion, and/or give their public comment. Members of the media will often rely heavily on the summary in preparing their pre-meeting and sometimes their post-meeting articles.

Some states have specific rules about what must be included on a table of contents or summary page. Even if there are no rules, common sense dictates that the table of contents should give sufficient information so the reader can determine the purpose of the item. Readers should know if the board is hearing a presentation for information only, planning to discuss a topic without taking action, or planning to take action on a particular item. The most effective method is for the summary to be written so the superintendent's recommendation is clearly stated. Districts that use "time certain" for some agenda items print the time on the agenda and make every effort to honor that time.

The public has a right to know about, and be involved in, the business of the district. The district and board must do everything to honor that right and keep their work transparent. Keeping in mind that the press tends to quote directly from the summary reminds us to be clear and unambiguous, reducing the chance of misinformation.

Sections for Each Division

There are two primary ways to organize the agenda packet: subject or process. The first involves having a section for each of the major district divisions: educational, business, and human resources. Districts vary in the terms used for those divisions, but each general area is represented. The second way to organize the packet is by the process that will occur in relation to it: information, discussion, action, consent, communication, and so forth.

A district may have other sections to include for a specific purpose and for a limited period of time. For example, if the district has embarked on a major technology effort, a section might be added for special updates on the project. Other examples include land acquisition, major construction or modernization projects, or a strategic plan review. For all these, having a separate section of the packet devoted to them may help create a wider degree of board commitment and community awareness.

Many districts keep the same agenda order for every meeting. If this is the case in your district, we recommend leading with Educational Services (sometimes called Learning Support Services or Curriculum, Instruction and Assessment, etc.) since the major goal of the district, student achievement, falls mostly under this division. When the agenda is organized by process, we think it is best to lead with items that have the most public and staff interest and that are the most directly connected to our teaching and learning mission. Following these items, rotating the other sections or processes may help ensure the same types of items are not left to the end of the meeting when people may be tired and have a tendency to rush through the remaining items.

Some districts have a policy about ending at a specific time; if so, the ending time and explanation of the purpose of such a policy should be stated on the agenda. If the board did not cover everything on the previous meeting agenda due to the meeting cutoff time, these missed items are listed on the next board agenda as "Items Carried Over From the Previous Meeting." Carryover items are dealt with immediately after the opening events of that meeting to ensure that they will not be left out again.

Individual Agenda Items

As indicated in Chapter 3, each agenda item typically includes the following: the topic; whether it is for information, discussion, and/or action; background; relevant information; fiscal impact; relevant strategic goal; and, where appropriate, the superintendent's recommendation.

We believe the actual agenda items should be concise and each individual item should be covered in no more than two pages. Additional supporting information, if it is not extensive, can be included behind the agenda item. However, if there is substantial documentation, it is best to provide it "under separate cover," meaning in a document that is separate, but accompanies the packet.

We should also note that many districts have a standard format to guide the preparation of any staff report. One such guide we saw required that the issue be defined, the history reviewed, any committee findings and recommendations noted, and actions requested of the board be clearly stated.

One small but important note: The person responsible for assembling the packet must make sure the page numbers on the table of contents correspond to the actual pages where the individual agenda items appear. Otherwise you'll have frowning and frustrated board members continually rooting through their packets for the right page!

SUPPORTING MATERIAL

Every leader faces the question of how much supporting material to provide in the board packet or in addition to the packet. What is enough? What is too much? We find the best practice is always to err on the side of too much information. One of the worst situations a superintendent can have is dealing with a board member who feels uninformed, not to mention the fact that gaps in information prevent the work of the district from moving forward. Such gaps also create a chink in the bond of trust between the board members and the superintendent. When you fail to provide sufficient information on a rare occasion, trust will not be damaged, but when you often leave a board member feeling vulnerable, the board–superintendent relationship is impacted negatively.

We recommend you send supporting documents with the board packet. We have seen board meetings where documents—sizeable ones—appear at the board table the night of the meeting. Board members, having no time even to scan the information and make an informed decision, become frustrated, even angry. Remember the "no surprises" rule? When new, important information is presented at a board meeting for the first time, it is an unwelcome surprise and will not be greeted favorably by the board.

Have additional copies of supporting documents available at the meeting for staff, public, and the media. Agenda items that have significant supporting documentation are often those requiring one or more meetings for discussion prior to the board taking action. Have supporting documents available for any item that will be discussed, even if it is the second or third meeting in which the topic is being addressed.

For board members, it is helpful to have a color-coded, numbered, or other system for aligning the documents that go with the agenda item. Do everything possible to make the logistics of the meeting flow smoothly so board members can focus on the meeting content.

APPEARANCE OF THE DOCUMENT

Take a look at your board packet—just from the standpoint of appearance, not content—and decide if it is attractive, professional, and reflects high standards and a sense of quality. Indications of quality include the following: font size and style throughout that is consistent and large enough to be read easily; clean, neat pages with no smudge marks or strange lines from the copying machine; and graphics that are appropriate and easy to understand.

How is the board packet actually held together? We have seen the pages stapled, in coil bindings, in folders, and in soft- or hardcover notebooks. Some districts have the divisions color-coded, tabbed, or separated by colored pieces of paper.

Readers do not stop to think about an error-free board packet, but they certainly notice—and comment—when they find misspellings, off-kilter pages, or charts and graphs that are difficult to interpret or seem irrelevant to the topic.

OTHER PRINTED MATTER

Information sheets or brochures welcoming visitors to the meeting and telling them what to expect add to the ambiance and tone of the meeting. Schools do, after all, belong to the public, and board meetings are the public's opportunity to watch their elected school board members hold their meetings and get things accomplished. Since members of the public have a right to speak at each open meeting of the board, Request to Speak cards are a must. You will want to give the same care to the design of these and any other printed material as you give the board packet.

Welcome to the Meeting

Members of the public appreciate a sheet or brochure welcoming them to the meeting and describing what the meeting rules are, how board meetings are run, and how they can participate. We recommend the brochure include a welcome, the names of the board members and superintendent, how the board is composed, and its legal responsibilities. The brochure can also give information about the board meetings, the time and place, an explanation of the agenda, and a brief description of how the board takes action.

A section of the brochure about how visitors can participate is your opportunity to demonstrate an open attitude regarding community involvement. This section describes exactly how the public can take part and give opinions about items on the agenda or an item not on the agenda. The brochure also is a way to inform the public about how they can get their questions answered or their concerns addressed outside of a board meeting—for example, through talking to the appropriate staff member and taking additional steps if the person wishes to pursue a matter further. Other information on the brochure can include a list of schools in the district; specific programs; and perhaps names of other staff members, their areas of responsibility, and contact information.

Request to Speak Cards

Members of the public have the right to speak at every meeting of the board. Most often, the time for open comment is toward the beginning of the meeting. We have seen districts ask for public comment right after the opening rituals of the meeting or just after recognition of students and/or staff.

Districts have options on when to hear public comment on items on or off the printed agenda. Some hear all public comment at one time. Other boards hear comments on items not on the agenda before the board begins the body of the meeting, and comments on current agenda items are heard at the time the board takes up that topic. Either way can be effective, but it is important to communicate the process to the public.

As we described in Chapter 4, Request to Speak cards are known by various names such as hold cards or yellow cards, and so forth. What matters most is not what you call the cards, but that people know they can speak and are aware of the process for doing so.

Once again, you want the card to represent your district's high standards. The card indicates what information you would like the speaker to provide. Be sure to have sufficient space for the person to write. Typically, districts ask for the person's name, residence, and the item the speaker will address, whether it is an item on the agenda or for general public comment. There may be a difference between what information you would like to have from the speaker and what is legally required. If you are unclear or have a concern, it is wise to check with your district's legal counsel.

Even if the information is in a "Welcome to the Meeting" brochure, it is helpful for the speakers' guidelines to be restated on the Request to Speak card. Potential speakers are often nervous, so simply knowing to whom they give the card is comforting. If there is a "hot" item on the agenda and there are many speakers, it is a good practice to have a staff member mingle among the people filling out the cards, offering assistance and collecting the cards.

Time limits for public input should be written on the agenda, on the hold card, and on the board meeting information sheet or brochure. Typically, time limits per speaker range from 3 to 5 minutes, and input on any one item is limited to 20 to 30 minutes. The board president may be authorized to adjust these timelines subject to the consent of the board.

ADDITIONAL CONSIDERATIONS

A critical part of preparing the board packet is proofreading. Proofread the materials, then proofread them a second time, and finally have a trusted, skilled associate proofread yet again. As writers, we tend to overlook errors because we know what we expect to see; a fresh pair of eyes can prevent the embarrassment of errors. The proofreader looks for errors, but also for reader-friendly language. If you use acronyms, be sure to spell them out in the first usage, remembering the jargon we educators use for our internal communication is not familiar or welcoming to those outside the organization.

Assembling the packet is important work. The superintendent's assistant responsible for compiling the board packet performs a number of important tasks: assuring consistency of each item and the overall packet; securing recommendations and signatures for those items that require them; making certain the table of contents is clear and accurate; and checking that the document is printer-ready with accurate page numbers.

To ensure that everything is in order and completed in a timely manner, the assistant must work closely with the departments on meeting all timelines. The assistant, along with the superintendent, is the final keeper of quality, making sure the final document is attractive and professional.

The district mission statement on the board packet cover is a reminder to everyone about the ultimate aim of the district. What is inside the packet should contribute to the achievement of the district's mission and goals. This is another reason to list the applicable specific strategic goal for each item. The packet itself is symbolic of the district's dedication to its students, staff, and community.

6

Communicating
the Agenda

Secrecy spawns isolation, not success. Knowledge is power, yes, but what leaders need is collective power, and that requires collective knowledge.

(Abrashoff, 2002, p. 55)

From completion of the agenda packet to the board meeting itself is another crucial time period in preparing for a productive meeting. As the saying goes in real estate, what matters is location, location, location. Comparable in board meeting preparation is communication, communication, communication.

Not only does good communication with board members and others help ensure an effective meeting, it also is the perfect avenue for the superintendent to display the skills of an excellent teacher and leader. Not only what leaders say, but how they say it, conveys a powerful message about the important work of public education, the goals of the district, and the priority placed on student achievement. As Albert Schweitzer said, "Modeling may not be the best teacher, it may be the only teacher" (DuFour, 2001, p. 16).

The agenda is communicated to the board and public in written and oral form. Both are important as a matter of state law and a matter of common sense. Once the "where and when" of posting is set, it becomes routine, a responsibility of an administrative assistant. As superintendent, you will want a set list of people with whom you communicate. Be sure those on the list who may have interest in an agenda item are made aware that the board will be considering the item. You also will want to be alert for any additional individuals and groups that might be interested in a particular item on the agenda.

Sending the packet is the first step in communicating; talking with the board members and other constituencies is your other, very critical responsibility. Surprises at meetings are to be avoided, and the best way to do this is by talking about agenda items with various people prior to the meeting.

DISTRIBUTION

Once the board agenda is printed, it is sent to the board members at their homes or businesses, depending on each board member's preference. Where and when to post the agenda is dictated by law. States vary in requirements about where the packet, or at least the agenda, must be sent and/or posted in order for the public to know what business the board is going to conduct. If you are new to a state, you will want to check the law and not assume the rules are the same as in your previous state.

States also have regulations about how far ahead of the meeting the agenda must be posted. Some districts have their own policies that exceed the state minimums and you must adhere to these timelines. Study sessions and workshops tend to have the same rules as regular meetings for when and where to post agendas. Special meetings, some of which are necessitated by emergencies, have different notice requirements. Be sure you and the staff person responsible for the posting are knowledgeable about these.

In addition to those specified by law, you may have other places you will want the agenda and/or packet to go, for example, to the leaders of the employee associations and to each of the schools via the principal. An increasing number of districts post at least the agenda, if not the entire packet, on their Web site. Many newspapers list dates and times of school board meetings and some also print the agenda. Cable TV is another avenue for some (usually larger) school districts.

COMMUNICATION

Board members are the superintendent's starting place. Many superintendents make a point of contacting each board member prior to the meeting; others respond to questions from individual board members. In addition, superintendents make sure they have processes in place for contacting potentially interested staff, parents, community, and media as needed. Each of these groups is unique, requires a thoughtful approach, and is key to the success of the district in meeting its goals.

Reviewing With the Board

Two things superintendents want to avoid: a surprised board member, and the sound of a board packet being ripped open at the start of a board meeting. This section offers our opinions about why super-intendents find it effective to review the board packet with each board member prior to the meeting, ideas about how to do it, and some cautions about certain practices.

The Purpose

Meetings are more efficient and effective when all board members are well prepared, when they have read the items in the packet, and when they understand the issues. The board meeting rarely goes well when a request for further information on an item is brought up for the first time at the meeting.

The purpose of reviewing the agenda is to ensure board members have all the information they need to be prepared for the meeting. These communications, whether in the form of a meeting, phone call, or email, are for clarification only. They are not to seek information about how the members intend to vote. They are not to persuade board members, but to offer your rationale for your recommendations, and to determine if they have sufficient information to make sound decisions.

Despite our best efforts, sometimes an item we present is not as clear or complete as we think it is. As a result, board members may need to ask clarifying questions or require more information. The solution to this is threefold.

First, the superintendent must ensure the packet is sent to board members with enough lead time so they can read the information and have an opportunity to ask their questions. Second, the superintendent must be proactive and set aside time for talking to board members. Third, a longer-term, overall approach is for the superintendent and board to have agreements, operating procedures for asking and answering the questions about board meeting agendas. Several states have sample oper-ating procedures addressing this topic, and some districts have developed their own. (Please see Resource A, pp. 146–149.)

The Process—Options

While the purpose of pre-meeting communication with board members is not to find out how board members will vote, the superintendents tend to know what board members support and do not support. They know this by becoming familiar with what board members care about, their interests and their concerns for the district. They also can learn this by providing sufficient time for comment and questions on key agenda items when an important item is first introduced. If, by the time action is required, you do not yet know how a board member will vote, you may need to reassess the ways you have been communicating with this member or structuring the board meeting itself.

Some of the board members' questions only need a simple explanation; other questions alert superintendents to issues requiring additional information. In this case, you provide new information or material to the questioner, and you make sure to send the material to all board members. Some superintendents, in fact, make sure the questions and answers to every individual board member's questions are shared with all members.

As superintendent, you must know each board member's areas of interest and expertise. This will help you determine when a member might want more in-depth information or be likely to ask more probing questions. Watch particularly for those individual "hot button" issues that are likely to trigger a major reaction or interest in a board member. The superintendent needs to be particularly diligent in communicating with that board member.

There are various options for communication prior to the meeting, and superintendents will want to know their board members' preferences. But first, both superintendents and board members need to be aware of the legal restrictions on the extent of pre-meeting conversations between board members that can vary from state to state.

In California, for example, a "serial meeting" is a violation of the law. A serial meeting is one where a board member talks either in a group or individually to a majority of the board in any way that could be construed as an attempt to influence action on a particular item. For example, on a board of five, board members 1 and 2 talk to each other about an item on the agenda. Even if they do not talk about how they will vote, neither of them may talk with a third board member or else it constitutes a serial meeting.

These legal limitations are for good reason. The board of trustees is conducting the public's business. Therefore, the public has a right to hear the discussion and debate, observe the board's action in person, and not feel everything is a predetermined "done deal." The superintendent and the board need to be vigilant and unbending in this regard.

Even though it may not always be possible for you as superintendent to prevent board members from having a serial meeting, you are responsible for keeping your part of the discussion legitimate while encouraging board members to do the same. These cautions noted, the superintendent may talk with each board member individually in an effort to clarify agenda items or provide additional information. Even some modified group communication is permissible as long as it is not with a majority of the board. One benefit from meeting with two board members at a time and rotating the members is they get to know each other better. A second benefit is that the superintendent and each board member have dedicated time together, which can be very beneficial over the long term in improving communication and understanding.

This system was very effective in one district until a board election resulted in a board that was philosophically split. At that point, one faction of the board refused to meet with any individual from the "other side." The main reason for this was that members of one faction wanted to talk with another member of their same philosophical position prior to the meeting.

The state's open meeting laws prevent a person from talking with more than one other person about board business. If, in addition to meeting with someone of like philosophy, the person was part of a meeting with a board member from the other side, it would have been a serial meeting. This meant that board members in the majority no longer wanted to meet with any board member who did not share their particular view. Due to the intense political nature of the board split, people were watching the board, just waiting for a violation. The solution in this case was for the superintendent to meet or talk individually with each board member. This solved the immediate concern, but further isolated the factions from each other.

Occasionally there are board members who see the meetings as an effort to influence or worse, manipulate the board. They are fine with asking questions if needed but do not want any pre-meeting communication from the superintendent that could be construed as intrusion or an effort to persuade. Our advice is to honor each board member's preferences, whatever they are, while finding a way to ensure that all are prepared for the meeting. An effective way to do this is through a board workshop on roles, responsibilities, and agreements about board meeting protocols, including the responsibility of board members to ask questions prior to the board meeting.

Good pre-meeting communication may not always be 100 percent successful. We are aware of one district with a board member who was losing interest in the board and district's activities. This member did not want to come to the superintendent's office or meet with other board members. Nonetheless, the superintendent remained committed to assisting this board member and keeping him from disrupting the district's progress, so through the board member's office manager at his place of work, the superintendent made appointments to see him at his office. It did not change the board member's interest in the district, but the full board knew the superintendent tried everything possible to work with this person.

Just as we educate every child who comes through the doors of public schools, superintendents work with anyone who is elected to the school board by the community. Quite frankly, occasionally there are board members who are wild cards, who are unpredictable. And we know of individuals on boards who purposely disrupt, create controversy and chaos, and even a few with dementia. These are very difficult people, but throughout it all, you must treat each one with respect and ask the board members to do the same. Ultimately, it is the voters who must decide who will be on the board, and you need to respect their choices.

Whatever the case, you must look for different options that will permit the best possible communication between you and board members prior to the meeting. When considering various options, remember this critical rule: if one board member asks for additional information, make sure every board member gets exactly the same information. Most often, sending written material is the simplest, using regular mail, fax, or email, and remembering of course that this is public information and may be seen by more eyes than just the board members'.

A second rule will also prove helpful. The superintendent needs to alert board members to possibilities of concern by a person or group over a topic on the agenda. Superintendents tend to call these "red flags" or "yellow flags" depending on the severity or intensity of the concern. If you learn that a group is planning to come to a meeting to protest a particular item, it is wise to call each board member with this information so everyone is prepared. This is an example of honoring the pledge of "no surprises."

Having board members blindsided is never helpful to the progress of the district. Board members prepared for the "unexpected or unusual" are not thrown off by a controversy and are able to thoughtfully consider issues and vote in a manner that advances the work of the district.

By establishing a pattern of preparing board members for the unexpected, the board will probably agree to communicate any potential "red flags" to you. Our preference is to have a protocol regarding communication between the superintendent and board regarding any question or information that could impact the board meeting and the governance team's preparation.

Potential uproars can often be resolved when a board member alerts the superintendent to a controversy, and the superintendent has time to act. You can talk with the individual or leader of the group that is disgruntled or ask someone on your staff to talk with the upset party. Many times an explanation, a clarification with accurate information for the people involved or concerned, can resolve the situation. At the very least, the superintendent has the opportunity to be proactive and to be prepared for the potential controversy.

A third rule we'd like to suggest governs board communication with others on the staff. Clarify whether or not board members can go directly to staff members when they have questions or need more information, or if all requests should go through the superintendent. The goal is to ensure that board members have all the needed information in a way that respects everyone's time and does not compromise the authority of the superintendent.

A common and effective practice is for the board members to contact the superintendent, who then answers the question or delegates it to the appropriate staff member. The advantage of this system is the superintendent knows what the issues are and can be alert to the possibility of a larger concern requiring that additional information be given to all board members.

However, the agreement in some districts is for board members to go directly to staff for questions in their area. In these instances, the staff members understand they are to inform the superintendent immediately of the issue, the dialogue, and any follow-up action. This allows you to determine if you need to send information to the rest of the board members.

Essential to the practice of a board member going directly to a staff member is an understanding of the line between requesting clarification or information that is readily available and asking for information from a staff member that will require significant work. Only the superintendent directs the work of the staff. Therefore, when a staff member is asked for something beyond easily accessed information, that staff person must not make a commitment to the board member to provide the information, but instead should indicate that he or she will check with the superintendent immediately.

One caution must be raised about communicating with board members via email. Each district should seek its own legal advice on this issue, but communication between board members and the superintendent, other than that covered by closed-session rules, is public. Perhaps the simplest rule is to never put in an email anything you would not want to see on the front page of the newspaper—or have your mother read.

The Staff

Members of the district staff are the second major group that requires good communication prior to the meeting. In most cases, this does not mean all staff, although there are rare times when it could. It means those who might have a particular interest in an agenda topic. These are typically the administrative leaders at the district office and in all the schools, leaders of the teaching and support staff associations, and individual staff who may be interested in or affected by a decision.

The Purpose

The potential for land mines is never-ending. Controversial issues are particularly ripe for misunderstanding, misinterpretation, and gossip in addition to reasonable objections and differences of opinion. This is when you will really need and value staff members who have an ear to the ground.

Communicating the agenda with staff is a two-way process, both from and to the superintendent. There are times after an item is out in the public that new information comes to light. This can be a piece of data a staff person came across, or the result of a telephone call or email from someone who read about the issue and brought forward an idea, article, or study that presents new information or a different interpretation. This is one major advantage of using the board packet as a communications device, for it offers staff the opportunity to communicate information to you after the publication of the packet but before the meeting.

When agenda items are put together, we try to provide the best, most complete information possible. The reality is, we can never have all the possible information, nor does the crush of business in a district allow endless gathering of data. If we waited for total, complete information on everything, nothing would get done. But whenever there is new, pertinent information that could affect the board's decisions, the superintendent needs to know about it and be able to share it with the board.

The Process—Options

Communicating with the administrative team is critical. Those involved in preparing the agenda are the ones most likely to be familiar with its contents and individual items. However, depending on the size of the district, there are many others on whom you rely as key communicators. Overall, it is useful for you and the leadership team to have a protocol for sharing board meeting information. Such a protocol might include a regular leadership team meeting preceding each board meeting.

Depending on the individual items, the superintendent and district office leaders will work with specific leadership team members. For example, prior to a superintendent recommendation for the board to take action on instituting full-day kindergarten, all the elementary principals and assistant principals would have been involved in the planning.

School site leaders learn about any last-minute thinking, and they in turn share what they are hearing from parents and staff. Prior to the board meeting, the superintendent may want to meet with any group that has a particular interest in an item. Such a meeting is another opportunity for teaching and learning. These communications further prepare the superintendent for the meeting.

Regular meetings with leaders of employee associations are part of the practice of effective superintendents. Communication and relationship building are the proactive behaviors of a skilled superintendent. Regular meetings create understanding, facilitate give and take, and prevent the buildup of big issues. Just as principals who are visible on the school campus, in classrooms, and in the teachers' workrooms and lounges prevent little issues from growing, so do superintendents who meet regularly with employee association leaders and groups. The "no surprises" rule works well for everyone.

The Media

Members of the media often get a bad reputation—sometimes deserved, but other times not so. When the superintendent and board get bad press, particularly for board meeting items, it may simply be the result of a lack of understanding on the part of the writer. As superintendents, we are not responsible for every negative story, but we *are* at fault for some stories when we have failed to talk with the press and explain the issues—particularly hot issues. If you fail to talk with the press when asked to do so, you may be allowing them to misinterpret issues, especially controversial ones.

Talking with members of the media requires truth-telling. If you do not want to talk about a subject, or cannot talk about it, just say so. Never lie. Reporters who find you telling half-truths or untruths are not likely to trust you again, and will bypass you on important issues, even those that might show your district in a positive light.

Avoid jargon whenever possible. Every profession has its own vocabulary, its own shorthand. We understand certain words, terms, and phrases because we use them every day. However, our "shorthand" is open to misinterpretation by people unfamiliar with this vocabulary. Some reporters may not be good about stopping you to ask what you mean, so take the time to explain terms, procedures and regulations, and the intricacies of the position or issue.

Take the opportunity to share the positive aspects of your district when you talk with reporters. While they may not use this information in the story they are writing, chances are they will remember what you said and write about it or allude to it at another time.

The school "beat" is not the most glamorous and is often given to young, novice reporters at a paper. Superintendents who remember their role as teacher are the most effective. Savvy superintendents also stay tuned in to a change in reporters and are proactive in inviting the reporter to meet shortly after the reporter has been hired.

One superintendent made a practice of taking a new reporter out for a cup of coffee and finding out about the person's background, interests, and goals. This is an example of relationship building—an important part of communication and good teaching.

This relationship building is helpful because there are occasions when it is very important for reporters to understand an issue from your perspective. In addition, the relationship provides you an opportunity to learn what issues might be of interest or concern to the public. The reporter's questions frequently are based on information, opinions, or questions raised by the public and/or the newspaper's editor or television station's manager.

Positive relations with the media serve the district well. When you take the time to talk with the key media people, you are being proactive, which can save you and the board many headaches and heartaches. In addition, when you have established a positive relationship with the media, they often will provide you with a "heads up." A reporter who covered a contentious battle for land acquisition called a superintendent two days before a board meeting to tell him that an angry group of residents living in the general area planned to come and protest to the board. This reporter thought the people were misinformed. Because the reporter called, the superintendent was able to call the leader of the group, give accurate information, and prevent the escalation of the issue.

Responding promptly to calls from the media is not just good practice; it is essential prior to a board meeting. Should you or a staff member ignore reporters, you can expect to see the results show in what is published. An upset or ignored reporter is never a good thing.

Talking with the press does require caution and judgment. One caution is that the superintendent should not speak for board members. One must be careful not to fall into the trap of discussing or conjecturing about what the board might do. You may need to remind reporters that your job is to present information to the board for them to discuss and take action at an open meeting, and that board members speak for themselves.

A second caution gets the "no kidding" reaction from superintendents, and it is this: While reporters cover school district stories, some are also looking for controversy and create new issues that make superintendents angry and take time away from our goals. However, it is important to take the time to meet with the reporter and talk through what occurred and why, setting ground rules where possible for further information and access. The reality is there are some newspaper owners and editors hostile to public education. Relations with the press will always be a challenge, therefore superintendents need to stay positive and proactive in the face of this ongoing difficulty. The school board beat is often not the most desirable, and sometimes reporters call the superintendent to get the information so they don't have to come to the meeting. Be clear about describing the board items, the background, the recommendation, and requested action, but stop there. Be informative, but do not do the reporter's job. And, when you find mistakes in a story, be sure you call immediately. For the most part, reporters will make corrections promptly and do not want to repeat them.

On the other hand, if a reporter does an excellent job covering an issue, send a thank-you letter and copy the reporter's boss or editor. Reporters probably receive even less praise and fewer "thank yous" than superintendents do.

TOUCH BASE WITH CONSTITUENTS

Communicating the agenda with parents and community members is often done more informally than with the board or staff. However, there are groups the superintendent may want to have regular contact with regarding the board meeting agenda. Those might include a parent council that is composed of a parent from each school, a bond oversight committee, or a coordinating council of various community leaders. You will always want to talk with the city manager, for example, about a potential board item that impacts the city. Being mindful of others who could be affected by district policies and actions is the key.

Parents

There are parents present at most board meetings. In fact, it is rare to hear of meetings where no parent attends. Some parent groups assign a member the specific responsibility of attending and "monitoring" board activity. That is one reason why superintendents and staff should pay attention to parents' needs and wishes as they develop policies and programs. The other reason, of course, is that parents provide valuable insights and perspectives. Besides, it is their children we serve.

Most districts have parents who are very active and vocal, either individually or as part of an interest group. These people make a point to know what is coming before the board and to state their opinions. Proactive superintendents make sure all parents are aware of actions that will affect them and their children, even when the parents are not vocal.

Certain issues will always bring out those parents who are affected. Count on boosters of activity and athletic groups to come out in force if there is any hint of a cut in those programs. A school board facing drastic budget cuts announced at a board meeting that it was considering cutting all high school athletic programs in order to balance the district's budget. The superintendent and board knew athletic boosters would fill every seat and the aisles at the next board meeting.

And that's exactly what happened. A large number of boosters came to the meeting with the intention of preventing the cuts. There were also parents and staff members who were trying to avoid cuts to transportation, counseling, and other programs. The boosters were vocal, but so were the parents who were concerned about the other potential cuts. As the evening wore on and the audience heard the financial pressures facing the board and district, an understanding grew that eventually turned into support for a parcel tax. If the parcel tax passed, most programs, if not all, would be saved.

Districts with active parent organizations at each school are fortunate, for they provide the superintendent with a simple way to stay in touch with the leaders. Savvy superintendents meet regularly with this group of leaders. They also know the heads of the various PTA, booster, and other interest groups and keep them informed about issues affecting the district, not just those with a direct impact on their specific programs.

For actions that may have a major impact on students and their families across the district, superintendents sometimes set up information meetings at one school or several sites that cover regions of the district. It is important to ensure that all parents know they are welcome to attend. The amount of misinformation that can occur about any change is phenomenal. You, as well as the parents, learn a great deal by being out and visible, answering questions and hearing what those affected have to say.

Some fortunate districts have an educational foundation that raises money for programs throughout the district. Frequently, the members of a foundation board are actively involved parents and community leaders. Not only do these people need to know about the district's goals, programs, and projects, they are an excellent group from which the superintendent can seek feedback.

Many parents are not involved in groups, so working through the principals with written communication is critical. Superintendents are wise to prepare the written explanation of any change and have the principals print this same message in each of their school's newsletters. No matter how conscientious the principals, if they are asked to prepare the information, there will be differences in the information distributed, and those differences lead to confusion.

A few districts, mostly large ones, have a Public Information Officer (PIO). As a professional communicator, this person can prepare written statements on many issues. A PIO can prepare a summary of the essential points for district and school site leaders and the board so everyone knows, and can speak to, the critical issues. This builds understanding and reduces the amount of misinformation.

Most districts, however, need to rely on an administrator, or administrative assistant, to do this work. If you need to rely on someone other than a professional PIO, providing professional training will be a great service to that person, you, and the district as a whole. There are excellent programs for school staff to learn and increase their skills in communications and public relations. Savvy superintendents take this training, too.

Community Members

School districts are not islands in the community. Other governmental agencies and civic and community organizations interact with the school district—or should—on many issues. A superintendent new to a community was invited to join a monthly meeting of community leaders. These included the city manager, police and fire chiefs, editor of the local newspaper, head of the city's redevelopment effort, president of the chamber of commerce, and the superintendent.

Not only did the superintendent become knowledgeable about what was happening throughout the community, the other leaders learned about the school district. All of the leaders had many issues in common, found ways to collaborate, and built support for each other's efforts. If your community does not have such a meeting set up, you might consider convening one.

Many actions a district takes affect at least one other community group or agency. For example, district safety plans regularly need to be reviewed. Clearly, any plan should be developed or changed with the involvement of each of the other agencies that have expertise, information, or who will be impacted in some way.

Service clubs and senior citizens organizations are other community groups to consider. The more people in these organizations are aware of district programs, the greater the likelihood they will support the district's goals and public education in general. We frequently remind school leaders that public schools belong to the public. It helps all children when the public feels they have a voice and ownership of the schools. Ownership begins with knowledge, and as superintendent, you are the lead teacher.

One effective strategy is for the superintendent to keep a list of key communicators in the community. Civic, nonprofit, and business leaders are obvious candidates for the list. Elected leaders at the local, regional, and state level are others. Add to these all the individuals in the community who care about particular issues and will take the lead to work for improvements. Keeping these people informed will prove beneficial in your work, so it is useful to review the list prior to each meeting just to make sure you or a member of your staff contacts an interested person or group if the situation warrants. A good question to ask regularly is, "Who needs to know this?"

Whether communicating with community members, parents, staff, or board members, your role as lead teacher cannot be overstated. All these groups need information that is accurate, clear—meaning jargon free—and straight to the point. If uninformed board members are a potential problem, so are uninformed staff, parents, and community members.

Meetings are most likely to go well, and the district is most likely to achieve its mission, if all the constituencies come to meetings prepared with as much information as the superintendent can provide. The better you teach others about the district and its work on behalf of all students, the more likely you will create and sustain those conditions that support powerful teaching and learning and improve student achievement.

PART III

Meeting Time

It is time for the board to do its work. This occurs in two types of meetings, the open session and the closed session. The open session is a meeting of the board in public, and the closed session is the time the board meets behind closed doors on a few legally permitted topics. Both meetings are times the board can make an impact, sometimes directly, but always indirectly, on teaching and learning.

In Chapter 7 we discuss the time just prior to the open meeting, the meeting itself, and the time right after the closing gavel. Before the meeting, you and the board members can begin to set the tone by welcoming staff and members of the public. The printed materials you make available for visitors provide information on the structure and content of the meeting and send an invitation to participate within guidelines.

When the meeting starts, it is time for the superintendent to take a step back and the board president to step forward to take charge of running the meeting, one that is the result of careful, thoughtful, and detailed planning. While this is the board's time, you as superintendent are alert and ready to assist at any point the president asks. Your attention to content and detail helps the board during the meeting and also contributes to effective post-meeting follow-up.

Although meetings can be stressful, they are the place for the board to take actions that move the district forward. Meetings are not just another in a series of tasks to get through, but a real opportunity to advance the mission and goals of the district.

Of course, while the actions the board takes are critical, how they do their work can be every bit as important. The tone of the meeting and the manner in which board members behave, the way they interact with each other and the superintendent, impact the district. Nowhere is the quality of board–superintendent relations clearer than at the board meeting.

There is a pattern to every meeting agenda. We offer suggestions on how to make each part of the agenda run smoothly: presentations and awards; recognition; consent agenda; public comment on items on the agenda and those not on the agenda; discussion/information items; and action items. There is even an opportunity right after the meeting when the superintendent can do a few wrap-up actions until the parking lot is clear.

The closed session is a critical time for the board to address sensitive, often volatile, and potentially costly topics, but only on those issues specifically allowed by your state laws. In addition to the content, superintendents and boards need to decide the best times to hold the meetings, who should be in attendance at the meetings, and how to keep everyone strictly on topic. An expert schools attorney offered suggestions to us, but our comments do not constitute legal advice. It is always important to consult your own legal counsel for specific opinions and guidance.

7

Conducting the Board Meeting

Everybody doesn't have to agree all the time, but you need mutual respect. It's also important for you to trust one another's word. If we want people to be collaborative, they need to be comfortable with one another's character and competence.

(Pritchett & Muirhead, 1998, p. 69)

Time has come for the meeting itself—the big show. All the planning by you and your team has increased the likelihood that the meeting will be another unique opportunity to achieve the teaching and learning mission of the district. You handled the pre-meeting logistics, planned the agenda according to district priorities, and ensured agenda items were carefully thought out and well written. Your staff rehearsed its presentations; you communicated with the board to ensure they are prepared; and you talked with other interested stakeholders about the agenda. You answered questions and anticipate additional ones that might arise.

In short, you did everything in your power to make the meeting go well. We emphasize that you did everything you can, controlled the variables leading up to the meeting, because once the meeting starts, your control over the actions of others diminishes considerably. But you knew that.

The meeting actually begins before the gavel is sounded. That is, there are actions the superintendent and board members can take that set the tone for the meeting and demonstrate the culture of the district. Once the meeting is officially called to order by the board chair, there are behaviors and practices that assist the board in accomplishing its goals and send signals to the staff and public about the direction of the district, the seriousness of the board, and an adherence to democratic principles. The meeting actually ends when everyone has left the meeting room and the parking lot is empty, not with the closing gavel.

Experienced superintendents know that no matter how prepared they are, the potential for something unexpected lurks around the corner. The unprepared superintendent can count on curve balls and screwballs; the prepared superintendent minimizes the likelihood, but is ready for them by listening and watching, and staying calm, professional, nimble, and ready to respond.

One night an anthropologist showed up to speak during the public comment section for items not on the agenda. He challenged the conservative board majority that had been sworn in to office just moments earlier about their desire to introduce creationism into the classroom. In another district, a rally of supporters for a charter school that started in the parking lot ended up in the boardroom asking the board to support their cause. It was a charter school in which one of the sitting board members had a financial interest, although he denied it. So, superintendents know to expect the unexpected. Every veteran superintendent has stories such as these.

Even though the unusual happens, we must be grounded in the purpose of the meeting, so let's take a moment to recall what a board meeting is and is not. A board meeting is a meeting of the board in public; it is not a public board meeting. The public is informed about the date, time, and place of the meeting, and has the right to speak at appropriate times at every meeting. The board listens to and takes into account the opinions and ideas of members of the public, but board meetings are not the time for dialogue back and forth with the public. There are other ways and times for that open dialogue as we have discussed in previous chapters, such as study sessions, town halls, or workshops. The regular board meeting itself is the time for the board to do the work of the district, to act on matters so the district staff can move forward to accomplish district goals to further student achievement.

The actions the board takes are critical, but meetings also serve a symbolic function. The public and the staff want to know what the board did, but they also pay attention to how the board did it. How did the board behave? Did the board follow the superintendent's recommendations? Were the votes unanimous or split? If split, why? Meetings involve a lot of routine; many also have drama.

Except for a few categories where the board is permitted by law to meet privately and out of the public view, it meets with the public watching. The meeting itself follows a printed agenda that has been posted in specified public places several days prior to the meeting.

In conducting the business of the district in public, it is critical to check with legal counsel about the specific do's and don'ts of your state. Because each state has specific requirements, nothing in this book should be considered legal advice; our text simply describes general best practice within legal guidelines and limitations.

BEHAVIOR

Whether intentional or not, how the board meeting is conducted and the behavior of the key participants send a message to the public and the staff about the quality of the district and its leadership. Observers of the meeting either gain a sense of confidence and trust or may begin to question the quality of the district and the abilities of its elected and selected leaders. Another way to think about this is to ask yourself, when the meeting is over, will the viewing public remember the actions taken by the board or the board's actions, i.e., their behavior?

We think the message should be intentional. For this reason we encourage superintendents and boards to think about each and every aspect of the public meeting, starting with the superintendent and board members' participation and behavior in the meeting and their role as a governance team.

Board members and the superintendent are watched carefully by the public and the staff, who come to learn what these board members value by observing actions as much as words. Clearly some board members think their duty is to question everything, even to be adversarial, in order to prove they are the "watchdogs" for the public.

Our view is that since these are "public schools," the superintendent, all board members, and the staff are *all* watchdogs. They have a responsibility to watch out for the best interests of the students and the public's schools. We are not talking about eliminating the debate of substantive issues; we consider such debates essential. We are talking about doing the district's business in a manner that protects the dignity of all participants, one that models the principles of good teaching and learning, civic engagement, and the power of the democratic process. The conduct of the superintendent and board members should be consistent with and reflect these principles.

Think about these ideas: "Children have never been good at listening to their elders, but they have never failed to imitate them." (Baldwin, 1961, p. 43). Or "Example is not the main thing in influencing others. It is the only thing" (DuFour, 2001, p. 16).

Superintendent

We start with superintendents, because you choose how you will behave regardless of the actions or words of any individual board member or member of the audience. In fact, once the meeting starts, you really only have control over your own behavior and words.

Of the other meeting participants, you have the most control over the behavior of staff because you have planned this meeting together. As a result, leadership staff should be very clear about your expectations. Board member behavior is less predictable, but is more likely to be productive if the superintendent has done the appropriate planning and communicating. Less known is how other district staff, employee organization leaders, or the public will participate or behave, but superintendents can prepare themselves and the board for dealing with the public in positive, proactive, and respectful ways.

As superintendent, you must stay alert at all times during the meeting. You cannot let your attention stray. Keep a positive, problem-solving attitude. Staying positive and listening with an open attitude is not always easy, especially when you feel attacked. But this is exactly the time when you must model the behavior you *want* to see, not the behavior you see. There are no requirements for members of the public to be civil. You simply cannot respond in kind to poor public behavior. Even if you bear the brunt of the worst possible behavior, never allow yourself to sink to that level. As Victor Frankl stated so profoundly in *Man's Search for Meaning*, only you own your attitude. It is the one thing no one can ever take from you (Frankl, 1984, p. 75).

Debates should be over ideas, not personalities. It is human nature to become defensive when a person who is typically difficult comes to the podium to speak. We suggest you try to listen to what the person is saying as if the person speaking were someone you deeply admired. How would the idea sound then? The goal is to evaluate the ideas presented, keeping in mind the district mission and goals, and not base your response on whether or not you or others like or agree with the speaker.

As we said, you must always stay alert to model the behavior you want, and so must your staff, especially the recording secretary or administrative assistant, for a second reason. To ensure proper follow-up after the meeting, you and your staff must have clear notes about what must be done.

The ultimate point of the board meeting is for the board to take action to move the district forward in a way that improves the quality of teaching and learning and student achievement. Naturally, you do not want board members to reach premature decisions, but at some point they do have to decide. It is unrealistic to wait to have every possible piece of information—something that rarely happens in our complex world. All of us in leadership positions need to have the best possible information at the time and then make the best possible decision for the time.

When you see board members beginning to rehash and circle back among their ideas, you might make a gentle suggestion—or give a note to the board chair to suggest—that it may be time for a motion. Or you might ask a question like, "It seems you may have too many questions to make a good decision tonight. Would you like us to provide you with more information before you take a vote?" Perhaps the board does need more information, but often a board member will say, "No, I think we have enough, we just need to summarize and vote."

Board members can get into the game of "one-upsmanship"—a particular hazard if meetings are televised! Knowing when to intercede requires good communication with the board president and political savvy on your part.

Board Members

The board–superintendent team needs to talk about board meeting behavior as a whole, even making it a protocol so everyone remembers the powerful link between board meetings and student achievement. Board meetings are not about "adult airtime." When parents, staff, and other stakeholders watch board meetings, they learn how a board operates. Observing the superintendent and board members' behavior, stakeholders come to understand what is important to each person and whether members respect each other and staff, or listen to differences of opinion with an open mind. Watching a discussion over a contentious issue is often the most instructive in learning how a board really operates.

There is a distinct difference between having opposing ideas over issues and arguing based on personalities or interpersonal struggles. Debates about ideas, programs, and district direction are healthy for an organization, but discussions that deteriorate into personalities are destructive.

Board members bring diverse points of view to various issues, and these can make an organization better or can push a district into disarray and confusion. Like superintendents, ideally board members model the behavior they want to see throughout the district. If we expect teachers to treat students with respect, board members and the superintendent need to treat the adults, whatever their capacity, with respect. When words and deeds match, overall confidence in the competence of the district increases.

Superintendents and board members who commit to not doing anything to make another member of the team look bad work together more effectively. Respectful behavior is the key. Embarrassing someone never pays off. It causes bad feelings that either create immediate problems or simmer and come out in negative ways later. Stick to arguing the issues and never make it personal. A reminder of the reality here: Two board members may be on opposite sides this time, but undoubtedly will face a time when they need each other.

Respectful behavior, or what might be termed "common courtesy," is the simple guideline. Effective board members listen actively and openly. They listen the way they like to be listened to. Board members state their opinions and ideas one time, not dominating the floor and repeating themselves as if others will not understand unless they speak at length, sometimes loudly and in an argumentative tone. Effective board members listen far more than they speak.

BEFORE THE MEETING

Whenever possible, the superintendent and key leadership staff will want to greet people as they enter the board meeting room. Often board members like to do the same. This welcomes people to the meeting, sets a tone of respect, and sends a welcoming message that you are pleased they are interested in the district and its schools.

Second, it allows you to learn why people have come and perhaps what they are concerned about, whether it is an item on the agenda or an issue they want to raise during the public comment section of the meeting. Since it is just prior to the start of the meeting, you do not have much time to alert the board, but anything you can do to give them a few moments to think will be valuable.

One evening, about 10 people no one knew arrived 5 minutes before a board meeting. The faces of two board members registered alarm. However, the superintendent had a practice of greeting every person, asking the person's name and his or her particular interest. Because he did this, he quickly learned the people were students in an administrative credential program and were there to observe a board meeting as a class assignment. That little bit of information allowed the board members to relax, greet the guests, and go on comfortably with their meeting.

Another time, when an assistant superintendent was greeting people at the door, he learned that one of them was mad about a curriculum matter. As the assistant superintendent continued the discussion, he determined the person had faulty information, provided the correct facts, and resolved the issue. The person who came in angry, went home satisfied.

It is a good practice for you and your staff to always greet people and welcome them to the meeting, but especially when there is a controversial item on the agenda. A handshake and a smile put a face on the district; they reduce the feeling of an omnipresent, distant, and uncaring district office—the "thems." It reduces guests' frustration when you are there helping them learn how to fill out a Request to Speak card and collecting the cards to give the board president.

DURING THE MEETING

How will the board president run the meeting, and how active should the superintendent be? Does this change depending on who is the board president?

General conduct of board meetings is determined by the entire governance team and memorialized in board policy. However, each president is unique, brings certain skills to the task, and will have ideas about how he/she would like to run the meeting. The president and superintendent must discuss each aspect of the meeting and reach an understanding so each can support the other in moving the meeting efficiently and effectively.

A superintendent worked with a board president one year who had difficulty keeping track of where the board was on the agenda and when to ask for a motion, get a second, and then ask for the vote. This president frequently was on the wrong page, fiddling with papers in front of him, and seemingly unaware of the general confusion he was creating.

Fortunately, the superintendent sat next to the president. Wanting to improve effectiveness yet remain unobtrusive, the superintendent had color-coded key items on her agenda and the president's and would point to them. She would also write page numbers on a notepad lying between her and the president. In addition, she had pre-written notes she could use as a prompt; these said "ask for a motion," "ask for a second," "this requires a roll call vote," and so forth. The meetings, while not particularly smooth, were definitely improved.

The next year with a new president, the superintendent moved the note "ask for a motion" over toward the president. He, with a little chuckle, wrote on the note, "I'm not Mr. X, I know how to run a meeting." Point well taken; board members come with different skill levels, and superintendents must adjust to them.

Preliminary Events

A number of regular activities occur at most, if not all, meetings. Every meeting has a call to order, flag salute, approval of the agenda, and time for public input. Frequently there are recognitions and awards, and also presentations either by students or staff. We offer ideas about ways to handle some of these activities to increase the likelihood that they will go well and will model good teaching and learning.

Recognitions and Awards

As we shared in Chapter 3 on planning, starting a meeting with recognition of achievements or contributions sets a positive tone for meetings. Many districts begin meetings by saluting people who excel in various areas or who give time or money to support students and the district's goals. Some boards like to have a student presentation or performance. You will either list on the agenda the generic terms "presentations, recognition, or performances" or the specific people and programs to be heard or honored.

Remember, the intent of these presentations is to acknowledge, reward, and recognize actions that contribute to achievement of the district's teaching and learning mission. There are a number of ways to do this.

The board president (or other member of the board as requested by the president) can announce the award or recognition before stating the recipient's name. If there is an explanation, it is helpful for you to write it out so the person giving the award has the essential information, along with a phonetic spelling of the person's name. With the growing diversity in the schools, there are many names people may not be familiar with, and stating a person's name correctly is a sign of respect.

When there are several recipients, streamline the process by asking the public to hold their applause until the entire list is read. This also eliminates the embarrassment that happens if one person has many supporters present and receives much louder applause than another recipient.

Expect a board meeting audience to be larger for awards and recognitions. Also expect that most of the people will not stay, but rather leave as soon as this part of the meeting is over. To preserve the dignity of the attendees and the rest of the meeting, it is effective for the president to call a short recess so people can leave before resuming the meeting. Before the board meeting, you may want to remind the board president to do this, if appropriate.

Recognitions need to be well done, but brief. Recognizing achievements is a piece of the board's business, but the board also has a great deal of additional business to do. If you and the planning group have done a good job of monitoring the number and timing of these recognition events, you will find this section of the board meeting positive and profitable in terms of generating goodwill.

Presentations

Student or staff presentations can be positive ways to begin a meeting. Students can perform or describe a program; staff can describe a program or achievement results. In either case, you want the presentation to be well planned and within guidelines you make explicit.

As we indicated in Chapter 4 on meeting logistics, equipment must be set up and tested before the meeting starts. We have witnessed meetings that were delayed anywhere from a few minutes to a half hour while adjustments were made. This does not please either the board members or the audience and does not model good teaching and learning.

Presenters also need to know how much time they have and that you expect them to stay within the time limits. We have witnessed an enthusiastic conductor, who because of the interest and applause decided to perform an encore, then a second encore. We have also seen presenters who were so excited about their program that they went on way too long. The enthusiasm for one's work or one's students is admirable, but the returns diminish when the other business of the board is delayed. If you cannot catch the eye of the presenter or person in charge, you will need to take advantage of any lull to extend your and the board's thanks, and indicate that the board must move to the business items on the agenda.

The Consent Agenda

You will recall from an earlier discussion that the purpose of the consent agenda is to expedite action on routine district matters by passing a number of agenda items in one consolidated motion. Again, it is an opportunity to educate the public that the board will expeditiously handle routine items so it can spend its time on more complex matters.

After reading aloud the guidelines for the consent agenda, board presidents typically ask the superintendent or the superintendent's assistant if anyone has turned in a Request to Speak card on an item listed under the consolidated motion. The president then asks board members and the superintendent if anyone wishes to "hold" an item, that is, take an item off the consolidated agenda and vote separately on it. If so, the item is pulled from the agenda and the member of the public can speak to it when the board considers that item.

It is the superintendent's responsibility to ensure that an item moved off the consent agenda is discussed and voted on at the appropriate time in the meeting. Also, as superintendent you will need to know if there are certain items the board is required to vote on separately and therefore cannot be part of a consolidated motion. States vary, but some types of items require a roll call vote of the board.

Heart of the Meeting

There are two agreements we believe are essential for boards and superintendents to make before ever getting to a board meeting. First, it should be agreed upon that the president calls on each person who speaks at the meeting, whether it is a member of the public, fellow board member, or the superintendent.

The second agreement is the exception: Only the superintendent calls on the staff. That is, the only member of the staff the board president calls on is the superintendent, then the superintendent has the option of turning to a staff member to respond. The superintendent reports to the board; the staff reports to the superintendent. Therefore, we believe it should be up to the discretion of the superintendent when to call on staff members for additional information or to answer questions.

Public Input

Members of the public have a right to speak to items on the printed agenda or speak about items not on the agenda. As discussed in Chapter 5, some boards hear all public comment at one time, whether the item is on or off the agenda. For purposes of this discussion, we will take the perspective of a board that allots one time for public input on items not on the agenda and hears public comment on items on the agenda as they arise in the course of the meeting. There are some issues that are unique to items not on the agenda. But first we will share some general thoughts about public input regardless of when it is offered.

The most important rule is respectful treatment for everyone, regardless of the issue raised or the manner in which it is raised. These are the public's schools and the public has a right to participate in the process. We need to model our belief in the democracy in which we live and about which we are teaching our children.

The president would be wise to review with the public the guidelines for addressing the board. If the board has a policy that each speaker has a maximum of 3 minutes on an item, the president should state this prior to the public comment and hold the person to that time limit. Fairness is important; the president does not want to allow one speaker to have 3 minutes and another 5 minutes.

Some districts use a light to signal the speaker when time is running out. For example, we have seen a three-light system that starts with green when the speaker begins, and after 2 minutes turns to yellow indicating the speaker has one more minute. When the light turns to red, the speaker is expected to finish the sentence, or do a quick summary and sit down. In other districts, the board president may state, "I will let you know when you need to summarize." You may need to monitor the time and to slip a note to the president as the speaker's time nears the end. Generally these methods work very well.

Superintendents and board presidents need to be prepared for the unusual, for the situation when speakers do not abide by the rules. There are times, for example, when tempers are hot and it takes a very firm hand by the board president to hold people to the time limit. Doing the least that is necessary, in the most respectful way, is always best.

Typically, the board president reminds the speaker that his or her time has expired, tells the speaker thank you and to please sit down. After repeated requests, some presidents use the gavel. We have observed situations where the president had the speaker's microphone turned off—obviously not an option when the district does not have microphones. When these approaches have not worked, board presidents have had to take more drastic measures. These situations include when a president called a short recess to the meeting and reconvened some minutes later. Another decided to clear the room before proceeding with the meeting and asked security people to assist.

Fortunately, these situations are quite rare, but they can happen over controversial topics even in the "sleepiest" of districts. Communication between the superintendent and the board and especially with the president is crucial, so the team can think through how to handle eventualities such as these. Clearly, this communication needs to take place prior to a board meeting.

The board also needs a process for extending the time for public comment. Typically, the board president has the sole discretion to extend the public comment time, and in some cases with either the informal consent of the rest of the board or an actual vote by the majority of the board. All of these processes can work. They simply need to be decided as part of board meeting protocol to which the board as a whole has agreed.

Items Not on the Agenda

There are some limitations on how board members can respond to items not on the printed agenda. Most districts have board policies that outline their practices in conformity with their state law.

In addition to printing the time limits per speaker and per item, printing the legal rules for public comment on the agenda makes it clear for everyone and avoids the perception of differential or even cavalier behavior by the board.

In your pre-work with the board president, you have established the practice that the president will read the rules at the beginning of the public comment section. Presidents who do this set a professional, businesslike tone for everyone and make it clear the president is in charge of the meeting.

The president clarifies the legal limits on how the board is allowed to respond to issues raised and why the board cannot discuss an item that is not on the printed agenda. When people unfamiliar with the process are given the reasons—that is, protecting the public's right to know and participate on all items that come before the board—they usually understand these limitations, even if they are frustrated.

To ensure the public sees the board operating openly and fairly, the board president should make it a practice to call on the speakers in the order the Request to Speak cards were received by the superintendent's administrative assistant. The exception would be if several people wish to address the same topic, in which case it is logical to hear all speakers on one topic in sequence.

When there are a number of speakers on one topic, it is useful for the board president to let speakers know that their names and topics will become part of the official meeting record, and to remind people of time limits per speaker and per item. Often, presidents ask the speakers not to repeat what prior speakers have said. Again, if these rules are written on the agenda, the board meeting information sheet, and the Request to Speak cards themselves, the audience will understand the parameters.

If your state law prohibits the board from discussing the item at that meeting, it does not mean the issue must come back on the next or a future agenda. In fact, most topics raised do not need to become agenda items. Speakers' comments during public comment tend to fall into several categories: asking a question; seeking clarification of something the person heard had happened or will happen; making a statement; stating misinformation as fact; and raising a legitimate issue that needs attention by the superintendent and sometimes by the board.

In general, there are several ways to deal with issues that come up in the open session, whether the member of the public is speaking about an item on the agenda or one that is not on the agenda, and all begin with the board president turning to the superintendent. If the answer is short and there is no debate or follow-up dialogue, you can answer a question or clarify information or turn to a staff member to do so. Of course, you never want to call on a staff member unless you are very sure that person has the answer and knows the rule about brevity.

If a question is complex or personal in that it pertains to only the speaker's circumstance, an effective practice is for the superintendent to ask a high-level staff person, perhaps an assistant superintendent, to step out into the hallway with the speaker to discuss the topic further and respond right then if possible. Do this in a positive way, so the speaker does not feel he or she is being punished, but rather is being responded to immediately and professionally.

Often, people do not have information or have incomplete or incorrect information, and a simple answer or explanation can resolve the matter. In other cases, by discussing the matter more fully outside the board meeting room, the staff person will understand the issue and can research it and give the person a call with the information at a later time.

Another way to deal with an item raised during public comment is to indicate that you or a staff person will look into the issue if the person will give his or her name and contact information to the superintendent's assistant before leaving the meeting. Board members must know it is not their place to follow up, nor should they automatically ask for the information to be placed on the next agenda. If you have proven your responsiveness and follow-through, the board will be confident you will handle the issue and let them know what occurred.

Follow-up is critical. You or the staff person must get back to the speaker in a timely manner. Responding does not necessarily mean the person will be satisfied with the answer, but he or she will have been listened to and will know you have followed up. You must then let the board know what the full issue was and what, if any, action you or your staff took. If the topic should come to the board, you will need to inform the board through a memo, email, or in a routine communication when it will be on the agenda. You or your assistant also will want to call the original speaker(s) to inform them of the date, time, and location of the meeting when the topic will be heard by the board.

Items on the Agenda

The public has the right to speak on any agenda item, but most items will not have a speaker from the public. When there is one, a typical sequence might look like this: The board president asks the superintendent to introduce an item by giving the background, the key information, and the superintendent's recommendation with rationale for the recommendation. The predominant practice is for the board to hear public input on an item prior to the board members' discussion of the item among themselves. Remember, this meeting is not an appropriate time for board members to engage with the public in a dialogue.

If any member of the audience has filled out a Request to Speak card, the board president opens the public comment time. This is not the time to call on people who raise their hands in the audience, nor for the board to call on people in the audience for their opinion. In fact, it is very rarely, if ever, the time to call on people who raise their hands, since everyone has been given an opportunity to complete a Request to Speak card.

As is the case with public comment on any item, the president is wise to verbally review the guidelines for addressing the board. Again, it sometimes helps for the president to request that people not repeat what a previous speaker has said, and that they stay within the specified time limit. As with public input on an item not on the agenda, fairness is important; the president does not want to give 3 minutes to one speaker and 5 minutes to another, or allow speakers to give their time allocation to one speaker who then can make a prolonged speech.

If your district uses a light to signal a guest speaker's time limit, as we mentioned earlier, it is appropriate to use this system for the public comment portions of the meeting as well. As with the public input on items not on the agenda, boards should be prepared for the unexpected—when someone refuses to stop talking, is rude or out of line, or talks about a matter involving a district staff member. Remember, any time a member of the public is called on to speak, boards need to be careful not to cut off someone who is talking about a matter the board thinks should not be talked about in open session, but is protected by free speech.

The fact is, in a democracy, we sometimes hear things we do not want to hear. Legal guidance is important, because neither the board nor the superintendent wants to turn heated comments by the public into a legal action against the district. This is a very tricky area and legal counsel is recommended. Some courts have ruled that members of the public are allowed to make derogatory statements about the superintendent or other staff members, but you will need to find out what is permissible in your district.

Sometimes the superintendent knows the line to draw, but in other instances you and the board will simply have to endure the speaker until you can obtain advice. In all instances, however, most superintendents and board presidents will try to dissuade someone from demeaning another person. A gracious and often effective response from the board president is a simple "thank you," letting silence and dignity by the board and the superintendent speak louder than any words.

As we have stated previously, there are rare times when the president may need to call a short recess, or decide to clear the room before proceeding with the meeting, or even ask security people to assist.

Board Discussion Guidelines

After all public input is taken, the president should make it clear that public input time is over, and now is the time for the board's consideration of the issue, remembering this is a meeting of the board in public, not a public board meeting.

When you have the exact wording of the motion written on the agenda item, it helps the board president focus the discussion. If the board agrees with the recommendation, a member simply has to read the motion as written. If a member wants to make a modification, the existing wording is there as a starting point.

We recommend this practice because we have seen agendas without the motions printed and board members struggle as a result. Making motions out of the blue is not easy, particularly if an issue is complex or controversial or there are modifications, failed motions, and the like. The superintendent's assistant, who typically is the board's recording secretary, must take careful note of motions and seconds, and will sometimes be asked to read and reread various wording. You will also want to take careful note of attempts at motions, as you are often the one who will take all the ideas and propose wording to accomplish the board members' goals.

One board set general guidelines for discussion that it agreed to follow, and these included time limits for discussion of individual agenda items. The board, of course, always provides for exceptions to its policies and does so in this case as well.

MEETING TIMES

As described earlier, some districts have a board policy establishing an ending time for the meeting. (Please see Chapter 4 for details.) If your district has an ending time, state the policy and procedures on the written materials the public receives. If there are people wishing to speak about an item on the agenda, and the time is getting late, it is a good practice for the board president to ask the board members to take up that item out of order rather than carrying it over to the next meeting. This is a matter of courtesy to those wishing to speak.

AFTER THE MEETING

After a meeting, especially a long one, our desire may be to head for our car and the road home. However, spending a few minutes after the meeting to chat with the remaining audience, perhaps talk with the media, say a few words to staff, and tell the board good night, builds good will.

Local customs vary, but we offer some cautions both for the superintendent and board members. One is for the superintendent to avoid standing in the parking lot talking to board members or for board members to refrain from standing and talking to each other. We offer this caution both for the appearance and out of respect for the feelings among various board members.

Remembering that serial meetings are prohibited, standing in groups after the meeting can give the appearance of talking about items that come before the board. The superintendent needs to be mindful of those who may feel excluded. We know of a superintendent who was held in high esteem by all the board members, but who suffered when one of the board members felt another was being favored.

With staff, we suggest you thank them for their fine work and encourage them to go home and get some rest. If a staff member was grilled at the meeting, you might spend a few extra minutes talking the situation through so the person does not go home with a negative feeling.

Be mindful of the staff and board members' time and good health. Our advice regarding meeting attendees and the board members is always to be courteous but professional, and when the meeting is over and you have exchanged some pleasantries, go on home. The follow-up that needs to happen can begin tomorrow.

8

Meeting Behind Closed Doors

Words are the board's tools. When the job is one of words, there must be discipline in the talking. That discipline involves what is talked about, how the talking occurs, and when it is done. It is not acceptable to talk about any issue that might come up. It is not acceptable to talk about an issue at an inappropriate time.

(Carver, 1997, p. 173)

School boards are allowed to meet behind closed doors to deal with certain topics. The terms for these legally authorized sessions vary, but the two major ones are closed session and executive session. We will use the first. Whatever the name you give it, it is a meeting of the board in private, out of the public view.

Laws vary from state to state, making it critical that you ask for advice from your legal counsel if you have any questions as to the appropriate topics for a closed session. We will not offer you legal advice but will provide hints, tips, and common sense suggestions.

Typical topics allowed by most states include some or all of the following: employee negotiations; student discipline; property purchases; real estate negotiations; matters of litigation that may be current or pending;

and personnel actions such as employee qualifications, grievances, and evaluation of specific personnel, including the superintendent. These topics are not open to wide-ranging discussion, but rather have limits specified in the law as to what can or must be done out of the public light.

Closed sessions provide important time for boards to consider topics that affect peoples' lives and usually have considerable financial impact. That is one reason board members are often referred to as "trustees." They are trustees for all of the district's business, but in the areas that can be discussed in closed session, where the degree of risk is heightened, the term "trustee" takes on added meaning.

MEETING TIMES

As we touched upon in Chapter 4, there are important considerations about when to hold a closed session. Typically, a closed session is held the same day or night of regularly scheduled board meetings. Occasionally, situations necessitate holding a closed session that is separate from a regular meeting. Examples of issues warranting a special closed session include litigation, employee negotiations, or the superintendent's evaluation.

When is it best to hold closed sessions? Some districts prefer holding them prior to the open meeting; others prefer after the public meeting. One district separates its regular meeting into two sessions, one for discussion, the other for action. These two sessions serve as bookends to the closed portion of the meeting. As with any choice, there are pros and cons to each alternative and you will need to decide which best fits your district.

Having a closed session prior to the open meeting often keeps the board more sensitive to the need to finish in the allotted time. We offer a couple of cautions regarding this practice. The first is to be careful not to create the impression that the real work is being done behind closed doors with open sessions serving to ratify decisions the board has already made.

The second caution is to be mindful of times when a topic is very complex and sensitive and simply takes more time than you first thought. This results in the closed session running over the allotted time. When that happens, there is a danger that the audience for the open meeting will become annoyed. A few minutes are one matter, but we have seen districts that delayed the open meeting by an hour or more.

To avoid this problem, some boards adjourn the closed session in order to start the open meeting on time and go back into private session after the public meeting is over. At times, however, this is not feasible. For example, difficulties arise when the session topic is a student discipline matter where students and parents, and sometimes attorneys, are present. Stopping a meeting like this in the middle is difficult, and board members are almost always sensitive to students and parents and do not like to make them wait in the audience or out in the hallway. Boards also do not like to pay the extra hours in legal bills when lawyers are waiting through the open session to return to closed session.

This problem may be avoided by scheduling the closed session for after the meeting. The consideration here is the fatigue of board members if the session occurs after a meeting that runs late into the evening, or after any lengthy meeting. Session items are almost always very serious and require fresh minds for considering and deciding weighty matters. Either way, it is a tough call.

You may want to consider a third option: holding a closed session in the middle of the open meeting, between information and discussion items and actions items. Unless students or parents are present for the closed session, the board can have dinner during this time. The same issue of sufficient time exists with this system as it does with closed sessions held before the open meeting. You will want to consider and be sensitive to the impact on staff, students, and the public if the session takes longer than an hour, delaying the move into open session.

Whenever closed sessions are held, there must be enough time to ensure the board can hear all the information and have a full discussion. That said, make these sessions as brief as possible. We repeat the caution that you and the board must be aware of creating a public perception that the board is really making its decisions in closed session, out of the public's view, and then coming into open session with everything decided. Whatever the option, it is important to take the time to reflect on what works, make changes, reassess, and continue to adjust where appropriate.

Space is another consideration. If the board meets prior to the open meeting, you need a confidential location nearby. Where space is a problem, the board can meet in the board meeting room after the open meeting is over and the room is cleared. You will also want to make sure there is a place where students and families can comfortably wait for the board.

CLOSED SESSION PARTICIPANTS

Superintendents, generally in consultation with the board president, are responsible for deciding what goes on the agenda. The superintendent also provides advice and/or determines who, besides the board and superintendent, should attend the closed session.

An important consideration is whether to have legal counsel present. While no superintendent wants to spend money, closed sessions include serious topics that require careful scrutiny and have costly consequences. Should the board make a decision without competent legal counsel, the cost to the district can far outweigh the money spent on a few hours of an attorney's time.

Often, very large districts have their own in-house legal counsel who generally attends all closed sessions. Most districts, however, retain legal counsel on an hourly basis. Some attorneys handle many aspects of school law, and districts contract with one attorney. Other districts use various attorneys from one firm whose lawyers specialize in a certain aspect of school law. Still other districts use attorneys from more than one firm. Some districts make it a habit to have an attorney present at every closed session; others have one attend only for specific purposes.

Boards rarely meet without the superintendent present. We think this is important because the superintendent must be present to offer advice and hear the discussion as well as any vote in order to carry out the board's wishes. If the board is meeting regularly without the superintendent or even occasionally, it may be a good time for the superintendent to dust off his or her resume.

An exception to the superintendent being present may be when the board evaluates the superintendent. In many cases, the superintendent is present the entire time, based on the philosophy that evaluation is an activity the board does *with* the superintendent, not *to* the superintendent. However, the board may want to meet alone at times. If so, the board needs to explain the purpose in a straightforward, honest, and open manner. The evaluation process must be clear and agreeable to all members of the board and the superintendent.

The superintendent also determines which, if any, staff members should be present. Some make it a practice to have the full cabinet attend, the cabinet being defined as assistant/associate superintendents or administrators who head up various district divisions. Other superintendents have only the administrator present for a discussion on a topic that falls within that person's area of responsibility. An assistant superintendent for human resources, for example, would be present to discuss layoffs or hiring of personnel. The person in charge of the expulsion process would likely be present during a board hearing or a review of a specific student expulsion case.

In the area of personnel, it is important to know specific laws as well as the employee-negotiated contract, regarding notification to an employee being discussed. Many states require that individual employees be notified that the board will discuss them. They have a right to attend and speak at the meeting and, if desired, to have a union representative and a legal counsel present. When in doubt, seek the advice of legal counsel.

AGENDA REQUIREMENTS

Superintendents are responsible for preparing the closed session agenda. Having the proper wording is important. Frequently, the laws governing closed session topics specify the exact wording you can use on the agenda. Some state school boards or administrator organizations offer advice on wording. If not, legal counsel can assist. You will want to be exact on sensitive issues.

We think it is important to list only those items the board needs to cover, not all the topics it is possible to discuss. Listing everything looks like a cover to talk about anything behind closed doors.

One district listed the superintendent's evaluation as an agenda item at every meeting. In fact, it was a catchall for anything the board wanted to discuss, since no board evaluates the superintendent at every meeting—if they do, the superintendent's tenure is likely to end shortly. In this case, the staff and public started wondering if the superintendent was in trouble because of this continual posting on the agenda. Inevitably, when there is a level of uncertainty about the superintendent, staff members start talking, taking their time and attention away from their work, away from a focus on teaching and learning.

Another area where superintendents must know the rules of their state is the reporting requirements for board action on closed session topics. There are some issues about which votes can be taken in closed session and reported out in the public session; others require the board be in open session when votes are taken. These legal rules need to be followed.

In addition, the superintendent needs to know the rules, if there are any, about keeping minutes of closed sessions. Are minutes required? How detailed must they be? Are you required to tape the meetings? How long must you retain tapes or minutes? You must check with your local and state laws to find specific answers to these questions, but general advice is to keep no permanent records of closed sessions not required by law. Ask your legal counsel about this issue.

There is a sound leadership rationale for not keeping minutes of a closed session. In the legal community there is a concept known as deliberative process privilege. Simply stated, individual board members will make better and more reasoned decisions if they have an opportunity to dialogue with their peers in a safe environment where divergent ideas can be expressed. The board, as a whole, makes the decision, but individuals can talk, explore ideas, and be thoughtful prior to the group decision. Detailed and discoverable minutes limit this free expression and can detract from productive decision making.

STAY ON TRACK

Savvy superintendents know they must be alert to closed session discussions that can wander from the few topics boards are allowed to discuss legally. Board members are more prone to wandering when closed sessions are held after public meetings and there is no end time specified.

All superintendents prefer boards where the members get along, respect each other, or even like each other. While this is desirable, it harbors a potential problem. Danger exists when board members get along too well. They can become chatty in closed sessions and it can be difficult for the superintendent to stop the friendly bantering that can easily move the board off topic. This is why we recommend having agreed-upon protocols for how the board will behave in closed session. One of those agreements is to restrict conversation to legally permitted topics. Closed sessions are out of public view, but are professional and need to be handled professionally.

Keep in mind that board members who are getting along well today may hit rough spots and end up on opposite sides of difficult issues, even turning against each other. We have seen this happen where a previously harmonious board became divided on one issue. Trust quickly deteriorated. One board became so antagonistic that the members began charging each other with violating the closed meeting laws.

Put simply, you do not want to play closed session cop, but from time to time you may have to protect the process and to help ensure the board stays focused. You may even want to ask the board to appoint one of its members as the person responsible for keeping everyone legal.

If you have protocols, you and the board can turn to those and review them periodically. If you do not, we recommend you get the board to agree to a workshop to establish protocols for how you will work together. We also recommend that you and all board members sign the protocols and share them with staff and the public. Some boards take the next step and agree to a Code of Ethics, which they also sign and share with staff and the community.

One protocol, and one part of the Code of Ethics, should include an agreement to keep confidential matters confidential. This may seem obvious, but "leaks" from closed sessions happen, are serious, are disruptive to the board and district, and put the district at financial risk. Pre-agreements about closed sessions will not stop a board member who refuses to follow the confidentiality rule, but they will give the rest of the board an avenue for dealing with it. And it makes this the board's issue, not just the superintendent's.

We also suggest a "no pillow talk" rule. That is, you have an agreement with your spouse or partner that you will not talk about closed session items. It is your own "don't ask, don't tell" guideline. That is, ask your spouse or partner (or anyone else you see on a regular basis, including staff) not to ask about closed session and agree not to talk about it. Sharing this agreement with the board and with your staff is also a good idea. As always, modeling is a powerful teacher.

There are many very difficult issues that we would be more comfortable talking about privately than in a public meeting. It is hard to have some discussions on controversial topics in public, but it has to be done— remember the public's right to know what is being discussed about the public schools. If you need a more pragmatic reason, it is this: The media is especially vigilant when it comes to closed sessions. The media tend to believe that everything should be public. Expect probing questions any time on any closed session topic.

So, how do you have discussions about other hard issues without the public present? You don't. Special meetings, study sessions, or workshops are one way to share information and have in-depth discussions. Retreats or workshops are less likely to draw public interest. The agenda should list the topic and state, "No action will be taken." Even though only those really interested in the specific topic might attend, always expect the public and provide time for them to speak. Avoid sending any kind of message that conveys a feeling of secrecy. Be sure to check any laws restricting venues for these types of meetings.

A school attorney told us about one superintendent who was very skilled in working with difficult and divided boards. He effectively used retreats, team-building exercises, and workshops to help the board focus on the mission-critical work. But he also understood the value of personal contacts with the board members. In order to build trust and increase their effectiveness, he regularly asked them individually, "What's the pebble in your shoe?" In addition to the less structured board meetings, he discovered ways to solve problems important to individual members. Listening to and taking seriously their concerns kept issues from complicating the public work of the board.

Boards require time in closed session to deal with certain substantive issues. It would be irresponsible to deal with something in public that requires the kind of environment that only a closed session can provide. As an example, almost any kind of negotiation, whether it involves unions, real estate, or a costly lawsuit, should be discussed in closed session.

Do not shy away from a needed closed session. Just be sure to follow the law and help the board understand the purpose and limits of these private meetings. Using these sessions for the right reasons, and not abusing their intent, will keep you and your board on the right track.

PART IV

Post-Meeting

The superintendent's job is far from over when the meeting ends. In fact, what superintendents do after the meeting both for the district and themselves can make all the difference in achieving district goals. After the meeting there is a natural tendency to let down, to sit back and relax. But by attending to a few important responsibilities you can continue the good work done at the board meeting and resolve any issues that arose. These follow-up activities are discussed in Chapter 9.

Having a plan to communicate the actions of the board is essential. Despite the attention some boards and board meetings receive, the fact is that a majority of people, both staff and community, do not follow the everyday actions of the board. Therefore, you need a plan for regular communications with each of the various audiences within the district and also the broader community. Those who are directly affected by a board action, and those who addressed the board at the meeting, require particular attention.

In addition to a communications plan, you need a system to ensure complete follow-up on board discussions and actions. A formal part to this involves assigning responsibility for following up on particular items, such as informing parents and student of changes in graduation requirements.

There is also an informal part to follow-up. This involves the human touches, the ones that build the district's culture and create pride and a desire in people to continually improve the district. For example, along with the formal notification, you might make personal calls to principals and key parent leaders about changes in the graduation requirements.

A topic too often overlooked, the superintendent's personal recovery and renewal, is discussed in Chapter 10. Board meetings are high-profile, sometimes stressful events. Districts deal with controversial issues and people with strong opinions on all sides of any topic. Sometimes the board is divided; sometimes media cover the meeting, heightening the drama;

sometimes meetings go until late in the night. Districts are responsible for what people care most deeply about—children, particularly their own children—so it is no wonder stakes are high.

Superintendents we know take the responsibility for students and their success to heart. They often anguish over decisions and actions that impact the lives of their colleagues and their students. This can take a toll unless you have a strategy for renewal and recovery in place. We strongly believe the day cannot be left to take care of itself. Rather, you must have a concrete plan for recovery so you can retain your passion and enthusiasm for your important work. Because you care about the welfare of staff and board members, you can discuss recovery strategies with them so they also continue their fine work with energy and commitment.

In Chapter 11, we acknowledge that sometimes, despite your very best efforts, things go awry. The fact is that we work in a context rife with political, social, and economic influences and ramifications. We think, however, superintendents have an opportunity to use the context to advance the district's mission, and so we offer seven thoughts about how to do so. We close by noting that we are all engaged in important, and honorable, work—work that makes a difference in the lives of generation after generation. For that, we are thankful.

9

Following Up

Equally important, if not more so, was our follow-up process. . . . It's called the After Action Review, or AAR. After every major decision, event, or maneuver, those involved gathered around my chair on the bridge wing and critiqued it. Even if things had gone well, we still analyzed them. Sometimes things go right by accident, and you are left with the dangerous illusion that it was your doing. We documented what we were trying to do, how we did it, what the conditions and variables were, and how we could improve the process in the future.

(Abrashoff, 2002, p. 60)

The gavel sounds and you think about going home . . . and you think about all the other things you need to do to follow up after the meeting. Often, board meetings are filled with invigorating and exciting events that feed a press eager for news, but these events are only a small part of the real work that takes place at meetings. When the audience has left and the press stories are written, you still have the budget, property, curriculum and instruction, and personnel tasks to deal with, because the board considered agenda items in these categories and took action on many of them.

One of our favorite cartoons depicts a boardroom in complete disarray with exhausted bodies falling from chairs while one participant says, "I feel a genuine sense of relief when meetings like this are over." While you may feel this way too, you have people to talk to and tasks to manage effectively.

Just as the time you spend planning and communicating prior to the board meeting is critical, so is the time you spend following up after the meeting. Your ability to communicate effectively is vital as you perform the formal and informal tasks that follow a board meeting. Once again, you have the opportunity to teach and lead; board members, staff, parents, and community stakeholders will watch you to see what kind of follow-up occurs as a result of board actions and requests.

Literally thousands of books have been written on leadership versus management and the difference between the two. The fact is that no one is a highly effective leader who isn't also a capable manager. Following up is an important part of both management and leadership. "Follow-up" is another term for "walk the talk."

As superintendent you are responsible for carrying out the decisions of the board. First, you decide what needs to be done, by whom, and when. Next you decide who needs to know and what they need to know. Your after-meeting to-do list serves an added purpose: It is another opportunity for teaching and learning—an opportunity to advance the mission and goals of the district.

We believe effective follow-up is based on a number of factors. These include the link to teaching and learning, a general communication plan that begins with behaviors at the board meeting and carries over to actions you take over the next several days, and specific communication and action steps for ensuring everything gets done. There are the formal actions, and there are also the informal ones superintendents take who are sensitive to the importance of human relations in this people-intensive enterprise, the ones that subtly build the district culture. Besides "cleaning up" after a meeting, many of your activities lay a good foundation for the next board meeting.

THE LINK TO TEACHING AND LEARNING

It is true that the board meeting is "the big show," the time when all of the sound planning we have encouraged pays off. It may well be the superintendent's best lesson on stage, but like all effective instruction, follow-up, corrections, adjustments, and reteaching are required in order for the board meeting to have been effective.

Using the effective lesson analogy, we know skilled teachers differentiate their instruction, not the curriculum, and involve students by providing feedback to them. The good teacher also reflects on the lesson, sorts out what went well, identifies which students need additional instruction or need words of encouragement, and then follows up immediately. Teachers who plan well, but fail to follow up effectively, cheat their students, who in turn suffer. In the same manner, when you fail to complete the tasks agreed to at the board meeting, constituents will have less confidence in the board and in you as superintendent.

We all know the damage that can be done to a school system if the staff or members of the public believe the words of the board meeting are not followed by meaningful action. Therefore, it is incumbent on you to design and employ systems and procedures to ensure follow-up and completion of tasks. As we described, effective follow-through includes both tasks that are formal and direct and those that are informal and indirect. Both are important. The latter may be very subtle actions, but they are very powerful as well. We define formal tasks as those required as a result of board action. While not required by the results of board action, informal tasks or actions, when accomplished, send a powerful message to various stakeholders about district values and norms.

To complete tasks resulting from board actions and other meeting events, we recommend boards and superintendents employ four strategies: alertness at meetings, systematic recording of tasks, timely communications, and consistent debriefing meetings and follow-up. The first two strategies, as we described in Chapter 7, must occur during the board meeting.

You will recall that alertness at meetings means that you and your staff must be alert and mentally present at all times. First, you are modeling the behavior you want. Second, you have to be alert to employ effectively your system of recording tasks in order to ensure accurate follow-up. You and your designated staff recorded what the board discussed and the actions it took. You also paid careful attention to the nuances of behavior of the board and people in attendance.

If these two strategies were accomplished during the meeting, you will find it much easier to accomplish the third and fourth strategies following the meeting, as well as the subtle, informal follow-up that distinguishes excellent leaders.

COMMUNICATION PLAN

Thorough follow-up, like every activity in a school district, depends on an effective communication system. We communicate in person to individuals and groups, and through various written venues, including letters, memos, emails, faxes, newsletters, and Web sites. We need to ask ourselves two essential questions: What information do we need to communicate and to whom? What is the best method of communicating with each constituency?

The first question has three parts regarding the people to whom we must communicate important information: Who must know? Who else would benefit from knowing? And who are the people that, if they were informed, would be helpful to the district? In general, those who must be informed are staff—the administrators and others we call the leadership team, teachers, and support staff. Others are stakeholders that include parents and members of the community, and members of the media.

Keeping all constituencies aware of the board meeting topics and actions is important. A frequent practice of many districts shortly after the meeting is to publish and send to staff and other constituents a summary of the board meeting in a one- or two-page newsletter called "Board Highlights" or something similar. Increasingly, districts are putting these board summaries and/or minutes of meetings on their Web sites.

Parents tend to read school newsletters, so they are an effective way to share important pieces of information from the board meeting. If there is a particularly sensitive issue, it is helpful to send principals a summary with the exact wording they can use; this creates consistency in the message each parent receives. We also recommend you establish a practice of having principals include the date, time, location, and key topics of the next one or two board meetings.

Computer technology will be an increasingly effective tool as more people have access to it. As with all district publications, whether print or Web-based, they must be current and accurate to be useful.

Staff

Following up with administrative and support staff requires the usual skills of effective delegation. Define clearly the task and timeline. It is also important to close the loop with the board, so they know their actions are being carried out efficiently and effectively.

In most districts, senior staff attend the board meetings. The definition of senior staff, cabinet, or the leadership team varies by districts, often depending on size, and may include assistant superintendents, directors, and/or principals. Exactly who attends is dependent on the superintendent's wishes or tradition. Typically, the superintendent and the senior staff have a debriefing meeting, usually the day after the board meeting, to determine the necessary follow-up. It is wise for the superintendent's assistant to be part of that meeting, both for the accuracy of information and resulting minutes, and because that person is the first point of contact in the superintendent's office.

A word about meeting minutes is in order. Laws may vary among states, but our belief is that minutes should summarize rather than narrate, reflecting the topics discussed and the actions taken. For closed session, the minutes list the topics discussed and any specific actions taken. If we just keep in mind that minutes are not the great American novel, but a record of the business of the district, we will stay on track. We have observed board members who had their feelings hurt when they read comments in the minutes, or where something one member said was left out. The longer the minutes, the higher the likelihood board members will spend time talking about the wording—not an effective use of their time.

Regardless of who attends the debriefing meeting, all staff affected by a decision need to be clear about what the board decisions were and how they will be carried out. Information is power. A well-informed staff is critical to an effective district, for districts are systems. Even an item not directly affecting the leaders of the teachers association could have ramifications for the teachers. Consequently, the district will benefit from having their thoughts and reactions based on their unique position and perspective.

Many superintendents meet with the appropriate staff the day after the board meeting to debrief the meeting and assign tasks. One superintendent meets with the total district office staff first thing on the morning after the board meeting to review what happened so the staff is fully informed.

Depending on the size of the district, the meeting may involve just you and your assistant or you and various key staff. Regardless of the number of people involved in the debriefing, what is critical is that you hold the meetings consistently to review the content and the context of the meeting. These meetings are vital for building morale, maintaining focus, and assuring that the tasks resulting from board action are accomplished in a timely manner.

A debriefing meeting that reviews the humorous, difficult, and confusing parts of the board meeting is important for reducing stress and building a team. Although you may not see the humor now, keep in mind what a motivational speaker told an audience of school district leaders, namely that they should remember that their failures today would make the best stories in the future. Superintendents know these debriefing meetings contribute to building a positive culture through good stories and sharing camaraderie. Both the team building and the planning are equally critical purposes of the debriefing meeting.

Together with your key staff, you will need to develop a list or chart showing the tasks, key dates for completion, and the person who is responsible for completing each task. Excellent tools and software are available to make tracking these tasks easier.

We have discussed "mission-critical" work several times; the work you set out at the debriefing meeting is mission-critical. You want to check for those small issues that, if left unattended, may cause your focus to be diverted or your attention to district objectives to be obscured. We believe and cannot stress too often the importance of your role as teacher to present the lesson and motivate others to do important work that furthers the mission of the district.

An area of special note is follow-up on closed session items. We noted the importance of confidentiality in the previous chapter. Those cautions hold true for staff whose responsibility it is to carry out personnel actions or hold discussions with lawyers about land negotiations or a suit against the district. As superintendent, you always balance the desire to communicate openly with your key staff and the necessity to maintain confidences regarding closed session discussions. We recommend you discuss exactly what you expect of key staff, including that they do not talk about closed session issues with anyone else, including their family members. Another agreement must be reached about not putting anything in writing, including emails, for it is all discoverable material in a court case.

The Media

Expect the media to be interested mainly in controversial issues, where the board is divided, or where the community or a segment of it is up in arms. We are all familiar with most of these: budget cuts, school attendance area realignment, school closure, family life curriculum, the firing of a popular coach, the latest snow day, and more.

Be prepared to respond to media questions on any issue that comes before the board. Even in the unusual case where a district has a spokesperson, a public information officer, it is the superintendent's responsibility to direct the "message." On controversial issues, the staff needs to be clear—media representatives are to be sent to the superintendent's office. If someone other than, or in addition to, the superintendent will be speaking to an issue or action, everyone involved should agree to the message. Speaking with one voice is essential.

Your message is always what the board decided at the board meeting. Whether it was a 5–0 vote or a 4–3 vote, the decision of the majority is the decision of the district and provides direction for the superintendent. It is not your job to comment on board members' reasons or motivations, but rather to speak about the decision and the next steps you and the staff will take to implement the action.

If a reporter wants the reasons or motivations behind any member's vote, you politely recommend that the reporter speak to that board member. Let the board members speak for themselves. Expect the media to probe further if the action of the board was not your recommendation. This is when you remember the job of the superintendent—to carry out the will of the majority of the board. That is democracy. Do not create a new story.

In the midst of all this, it is good to remind yourself how important it is for the media to report the positive news about district successes. Always work on building those relations with the media, encouraging them to focus on the good things your district is doing for children as well as the "sensational."

Other Stakeholders

In addition to staff and parents, you will want to communicate with other stakeholders depending on the topics the board is considering. The business community is one of these stakeholders. Remembering school districts are often among the largest businesses in the community, as CEO you will want to connect with leaders of other businesses.

Then there are those groups and individuals you consider as part of the category of "good neighbors." As an example, some board actions might require formal follow-up with the city manager or fire chief. Others might involve contacting the neighbors in an area where school construction is being scheduled. The saying about "an ounce of prevention" is a good guideline. Being a good neighbor is simply a matter of good communication.

Some board actions require formal communication from the superintendent, yet most often these tasks are delegated to key staff. For example, you must formally notify a business that won a competitive bid: the university that was approved to place student teachers or the architecture firm selected to design your next building project. Even though appropriate staff members will handle the details of carrying out board actions, it is the superintendent's responsibility to ensure this is done.

We have heard, occasionally, of superintendents assuming someone else in the organization wrote the appropriate letter, and who later paid a heavy price when the formal communication did not occur. As head of the district, make sure your key staff know how important it is to send the right letters in a timely manner. Most letters go out with your signature, with a copy sent to the department leader who is responsible for overseeing the performance of the provider of services or products.

Whether it is required or not, we also suggest you send a formal letter to the unsuccessful bidders. Simply thanking people for their interest in the district and their willingness to take the time and expense to prepare and submit a proposal is courteous, good business, and helps in establishing respectful relationships with community stakeholders.

FORMAL FOLLOW-UP

Board meetings cover many topics and affect people in different ways. Thinking through what you need to do in a systematic manner ensures you do not miss anything. One system is for you and your key leaders to work through the meeting agenda in the order it occurred, think about what happened in each part and who is or will be affected. For example, review what happened regarding recognition and awards, and determine if any follow-up is necessary or just nice to do. Next, review public comment on items not on the agenda, then discussion items without action, action items with or without public comment, and board member comments and requests.

In addition to the intended consequences, it is always wise for your team to include a discussion of any unintended consequences. What might be the fallout or reaction to a board decision and who could be affected in addition to the obvious? One practice is to have a list of the key stakeholders and review the list along with each decision to be sure no one has been overlooked.

For example, a change in bus schedules obviously affects the transportation department, the schools, and the students and parents. But this shift in the daily schedule likely will also affect food services, maintenance and operations, area childcare providers, after school recreation teams, and others. Will the lunch periods change? Can lawn mowing begin at 2:30 p.m. instead of 3:00? Might there be an impact on the hours people will need to work? A shift in schedule is always of interest to the employee associations. If you did not cover this in the planning sessions, now is the time.

Recognition, Awards, Presentations

Recognition of students, staff, parents, and community members often comes first in a board meeting and occasionally requires follow-up. If someone being recognized could not attend, provision must be made for getting the certificate or plaque delivered. At times, publicity may be in order through the board meeting summary, district newsletter, district Web page, or in the local press.

An individual or group who made a presentation may have raised some questions in board members' minds, so you may need to provide follow-up information. A member of the media may contact you for additional insight or information. As always, remember your response may reach many people.

Public Comment—Non-Agenda Items

Frequently, public comment on items not on the agenda comes next in the meeting, before the business on the posted agenda. Depending on the nature of the public comment, the superintendent may need to follow up with information via telephone, in person, or through delegating to the appropriate staff. If delegating, it is important that the member of the public knows that you, the superintendent, asked the staff member to call because of his or her direct involvement in the issue. You do not want the person to feel like you "handed him off" on someone else.

When following up, you often find a person who needs information, wants to know with whom to communicate, or simply wants to vent. Remember Jan Carlzon (1987), former president and engineer of the turnaround of Scandinavian Airlines, who said in *Moment of Truth* that you have 15 seconds to win people over or alienate them further. We agree. Even though people may be upset or angry, you have an opportunity to win them over.

Listening is the key. Sometimes that is all it takes, but careful listening allows us to determine the real concern and find a solution or explain why we cannot do what is asked. Along with listening, using clear language, not educationeze, is our best tool.

Remember to follow up with the board. For every person who spoke at the meeting, let the board know what actions occurred as a result of the communication. If no action was necessary, still let the board, and of course, the person, know you heard what was said.

Information/Discussion Items

Some board agenda topics are for information or discussion only and do not require any further action on your part. They are on the agenda for informing the board about district programs or issues and allowing members to discuss them as a group. At times these discussions lead to a request for additional information or become topics for future action. These are the items we discuss in the next section as "two-meeting rule" topics, which are for information and discussion at one board meeting and for action at the next or a future meeting.

We think careful planning and placement of information and discussion items on board agendas is valuable. As superintendent, you want to continually build board members' knowledge of the district, its programs, data for future decision making, and educational trends. A knowledgeable board is a more effective board. By discussing matters of importance, the superintendent and board demonstrate and model their belief in continuous learning. It also keeps the district focused on what is important, not just what is urgent.

Action Items Require Follow-Up

Many board actions are routine: pay the warrants, approve the purchase orders, hire the staff, and so forth. The follow-up on these also should be routine, but it is a good idea to check periodically to see how quickly and efficiently these routine items are completed. Many school districts have a reputation for being slow on paying bills; these kinds of problems are easily rectifiable when you know and can reevaluate systems and practices with your team.

With regard to non-routine action items, we recommend the superintendent meet with those responsible to make sure that the necessary steps will be taken. Be sure the responsible person is clear about what must be done and whether additional follow-up with the board may be necessary, reporting any such information to you.

Then there are those board decisions that have widespread effect. These can be an addition, a deletion (unfortunately rare), or a change in board policy, adoption of new curricula or curriculum materials, an increase in the price of student lunches, or a reorganization of the district leadership structure. Those board actions affecting the direction of the district take highest priority and require careful thought about communication: to whom, when, and how. You need systems in place to make the changes and to ensure full communication.

Those critical items that were for discussion only the first time, and are likely to return for further discussion and eventual action, deserve special time and attention. The superintendent and staff must listen carefully to the community input and board thoughts and ideas during this initial discussion. Their comments, questions, and ideas provide direction for how to prepare the item for action.

In some cases, the item will appear on the second meeting agenda exactly as written the first time; other times you will make changes based on the board discussion. Or it may be that the item needs to be withdrawn for a period of time for additional research. Some superintendents do not put a recommendation on the first reading, but do on the second reading when the board is asked to take action.

Board Member Requests

This is a serious and often confusing issue for superintendents. To effectively carry out the board's wishes, you have to be clear about what it is that constitutes direction for preparation of an agenda item requested for the first time during a board meeting, generally under "board member reports." Some districts have a policy indicating at least two board members must support an item for the next or future agenda. However, that often does not resolve the underlying issue of priorities and time, because it is rare for a board member not to get support from at least one other board member. After all, if a member wants support down the road, he or she better support a colleague's request now.

This is when having a clear mission statement with specific goals helps keep everyone focused on what matters. So does the 12-month calendar. Including the 12-month calendar in each board packet is a tool that allows the superintendent, or a board member, to draw the board's attention to the planned priorities. Resources, both time and money, are finite. If the board is committed to the goals it set out for the year, everyone must be vigilant in protecting the resources to fulfill the goals. Each new "gee, I think this would be interesting" takes staff away from their focus on the established goals, which is frustrating.

We all learn about promising programs and hear new ideas from colleagues, conferences, or the newspaper, and they may sound wonderful. It is easy to get into the trap of thinking we are not doing enough for our students. Superintendents are as guilty of this as board members! One must remember, however, that another district's wonderful program is one thing they are doing, and they may not be doing some of the wonderful things your district is doing.

Doing anything well requires focus—"laser-like" focus is the current term. This is where board members as well as superintendents need to monitor themselves and each other, asking, "How does this help us achieve our stated goals?" and "If we ask staff to do this, what will they not have time to do?"

These are tough questions, but effective boards and superintendents ask these of themselves. This is another good reason to have the mission and goals posted in the boardroom and on the board packet. We all need reminders to stay focused, to stay the course.

Building the Next Meeting Agenda

Each board meeting contains the building blocks for the next board agenda. Your key leadership staff and administrative assistant are your best eyes and ears as they record the tasks during the meeting, and then implement actions taken by the board and prepare for the next meeting.

In a planning meeting, you and these key staff rough out the next agenda. Included in your discussion are any carryover items, those the board could not address in the allotted meeting time, and discussion topics that now require action. Other meeting topics are follow-up on communications at the last meeting, items listed on the 12-month calendar, recognitions and awards, presentations, and special committee reports.

Evaluating the Board Meeting

Superintendents and boards who are committed to being as effective as possible take time periodically to evaluate the meetings. Of particular importance is reviewing how the board is doing with regard to its mission-critical work. One district had a rating sheet board members filled out at the end of each meeting. At first this was helpful but then it became so routine it lost its meaning.

We believe a better practice is to hold at least one annual workshop to review how the board, and the board and superintendent team, is doing. Focusing on the protocols adopted by the board to guide its work is a valuable activity. We take stock of what we are doing, how we are doing it, and ask what we could do to be better. Checking ourselves against what we said we would do demonstrates accountability at the highest level. Just as we set high standards for students, so should we set high standards for ourselves.

INFORMAL TASKS

At a conference, we heard a superintendent tell his colleagues, "Well, I was so disgusted with the person's conduct at the meeting, I just decided

I would not respond to him ever again." We understand the anger, but we do not think it is acceptable to behave in this manner. Instead, we recommend taking a few minutes before responding to people who in board meetings express an unpopular opinion or take a minority position on an issue. Thanking someone for expressing an opinion is not the same as agreeing.

We often hear members of the public say, "I have never spoken to the board before and I am a little nervous." Remember, it takes courage to come to a public meeting and express an opinion. Without question we sometimes hear people express opinions that are outrageous, uninformed, or illogical. These are the times when we call on our good teaching skills to remain calm, stay focused on our mission, and promote the work of the district.

You may not feel like it, but writing a simple note affirming a person's attendance at the meeting is helpful in building a future relationship with someone who might otherwise feel disenfranchised. You are not agreeing or disagreeing with the substance of the position, rather you are reaching out to someone who cared enough about an issue to come to a meeting.

On the all too rare occasion when someone comes forward to thank or praise the board or superintendent or some member of the district, take the time to call or write a quick thank-you note. Honest praise is an effective strategy to reinforce and reward behavior.

Writing notes is what we call an informal action; that is, they are not required as a result of board action, rather they are the result of responding with sensitivity to the human conditions inherent in the meeting.

Many effective superintendents tell us about the appreciation they receive as a result of sending an honest and sincere note of thanks or commendation, making a telephone call after the meeting to a staff member at home, or taking time the next day to deal with the "people issues" that result from the meeting.

Some superintendents perform other informal actions after a situation that unfortunately seems to occur too frequently: A member of the superintendent's staff is criticized or taken to task by a trustee or a member of the public during a meeting. If it was a board member, we believe the superintendent must talk with that member soon after the meeting, in private, to discuss the impact of this behavior and agree on a different approach. Even if the board member regrets the behavior and apologizes to a staff member, the apology tends to be in private while the rude behavior was in public. That is a gap that is hard to bridge.

We also believe it is important for you to provide support or direction for the staff person as soon as possible following the meeting. This is the superintendent's responsibility, not one to delegate to anyone else in the organization.

Times like these are informal opportunities to teach through encouragement and direction. When you provide support to staff members who have been criticized, you send a very subtle, but very powerful message that you value and will assist them. Your staff will be willing to take risks knowing that they have your backing, even when correction and redirection is needed. Giving guidance in an encouraging, problem-solving manner lifts people and inspires them to do better.

Thank-you notes, telephone calls, emails, and personal visits are all tasks that are not required, but are kind, thoughtful actions. They also are opportunities to model the culture you want and set the tone for behavior of each person's interactions with others throughout the district. Respect for all begins with the superintendent.

We encourage you to stop by a school to thank a teacher who came to the meeting or to show appreciation for students who made a presentation. Not only will the students in the seventh-grade jazz band be pleased you came by to thank and praise them, you will feel a glow and be reminded of why you love this important work.

Superintendents' reputations are built ultimately on what they do, not what they say. Actions must match words and the board must see their decisions are carried out effectively and efficiently. The formal tasks are critical for progress; the informal tasks are essential for building a culture where people do their best work.

10

Recovering

"A spouse who listens carefully while I replay the night . . ."

"A cold bottle of Moosehead Beer . . ."

"A welcome from my cat who could care less what I did before I got home . . ."

(Colleague superintendents)

After the big game, the tough final examination, the performance where you remembered every line, or a challenging board meeting, there is a sense of exhilaration, exhaustion, and relief. The need to decompress following the meeting is rarely discussed, but we believe it is essential to consider if the superintendent is to maintain a balanced perspective on leadership and life. Runners take time after the race to cool down and stretch, deep sea divers come up slowly, and authors take occasional breaks after writing for long periods. These are planned recovery times; superintendents also need recovery plans. This is particularly important after stressful, anxiety-producing, and difficult board meetings.

At a board meeting, leaders must be present, alert, and focused. Paying close attention is essential, and it is demanding and even tiring. This translates into the need to allow for—and plan for—a period of recovery following the meeting. This is not an offhand recommendation. We firmly believe district effectiveness is enhanced when superintendents are in good health, rested, and able to maintain a positive outlook, especially during challenging times—and these are challenging times! The same can be said for staff members who have been "on point" at the meeting, and for board members themselves.

Board meetings range from calm, quiet, and routine businesslike events to those that require security officers to keep the peace. Many meetings are stressful because of the importance of the issues, the level of interest from various stakeholders, and media coverage. Even meetings that seem routine require the participants' full attention, which takes energy and stamina. We have yet to meet a superintendent who does not express a sense of anxiety before board meetings, basically because of the unknown. We never can be sure what will happen at a board meeting.

Emotions often run high because the issues are important and occasionally controversial. After all, the board makes decisions that affect the future of children, and parents and staff who care deeply about these children. Many issues concern local government and community agencies and the broader community, such as when the district is buying land for a new school or putting a bond measure on the ballot. The stakes are always high because, fortunately, school districts matter to a community.

In the previous chapter, we discussed the professional follow-up actions the superintendent takes after the board meeting is over that are critical to the district's progress. The personal side of "after the meeting" is also important. The night of and the day after the board meeting should not be left to chance or just become another day on the job. In the same way you decide consciously what actions will be helpful to the district, you should do the same for yourself. Far too many people forget to take care of themselves. Remember to take care of your own well-being—sacrificing yourself to the district is not a good long-term, or even short-term, strategy.

Take care of yourself. You, in fact, are the only one who can. Once again, you have an opportunity to teach and to model healthy living for others in the organization. Your values are on display. If you assert that the district believes in strong families, but you never find time for your own family, the district value is hollow. If you tell staff their fitness is important, but you are at the office every day for 12 or 14 hours, neglecting to get exercise or eat right, the staff gets the true message about what you really value.

We learned this in part the hard way through the times in our own lives when we did not pay attention to the importance of recovery. The end result was generally negative, not only for our health but for others in our family and at work. We learned it from our colleagues whom we watched at times become sick or encounter periods of depression.

The book and movie *Fish*, a wonderful study of the power of organizational climate and positive employee attitude, is a reminder of this notion of perspective and choice. The positive attitude of the workers at the Seattle Pike Place Fish Market is infectious for their colleagues and their customers.

The workers say, "Be there," meaning be fully present at what you are doing. They also point out that we get to choose our attitude. If we lose our positive attitude and enthusiasm for our work, we will not be as effective and, chances are, neither will our co-workers. Children deserve our best. We need to be there for them with our positive attitude; nothing less will do. The recovery period is important because it helps us maintain the enthusiasm we must have for our work. And it begins right after the meeting.

IMMEDIATELY AFTER THE MEETING

In workshops we conduct on effective board meetings, we ask our colleagues to tell us what they do right after the meeting. Almost none find they can go right home and go to bed, even after a meeting that lasted into the wee hours of the next morning. A few of their responses were at the beginning of this chapter. Here is a longer version of the list.

- Reading the newspaper and having a bowl of cereal
- Enjoying a Moosehead beer and some chocolate chip cookies
- Reading the comics in the newspaper
- Doing a half hour on the treadmill
- Having a glass of chardonnay and a bowl of goldfish crackers
- Watching a slapstick movie
- Immersing oneself in a gripping novel
- Going out with the cabinet for pie and coffee
- Playing with one's dog or cat
- Spending time with one's children—if they are still awake
- Reading Dave Barry columns
- Fixing a bowl of grits and washing it down with a scotch

Whatever *your* routine, it is important to have some way to unwind, to put life into perspective. Start by doing your own survey. Ask your fellow superintendents and your board members what their favorite unwinding activities are. You might find something new that will work for you.

THE NEXT DAY

In addition to right after the meeting, it is helpful to have a "morning after" plan. Some superintendents go right to the office and begin working on board meeting follow-up tasks. Others hold a meeting with staff. Still others like to do something else, like visit a school to read to students. Our suggestion is to do the latter, particularly after a difficult meeting.

Many superintendents we know have a school visit scheduled the morning after every board meeting, and do not permit anything to interfere with it. Going immediately to a school, seeing children learning and teachers teaching, is renewing. It reminds you about the purpose—the goal of this very important work—and why you wanted to be a superintendent in the first place. Nothing quite compares to reading with a first grader, or watching a group of middle school students collaborate on a project, or listening to high school students debate a current political issue. Kids are restorative. So are our fine teachers.

If you choose to have a staff meeting, frame it as a recovery activity for yourself and the staff. Even though you have business to conduct, include lighter moments and use it for team building. One superintendent we know inherited a tradition of having the entire district office staff (except someone to answer the telephone) come together the first thing on the morning after a board meeting. The purpose was for the superintendent and cabinet to review the agenda and share the board's actions. This proved to be a good opportunity to communicate, build morale, and keep the focus on teaching and learning.

In another district, the superintendent held a breakfast debriefing meeting with the cabinet. She used it as an opportunity to build team and increase collaboration between the administrators and to coordinate their goals and projects.

THE LONG VIEW

The time immediately after the board meeting is one small part of taking care of yourself. The bigger picture is your overall health—physically, emotionally, intellectually, and spiritually. In addition to the district family, you have your own family and personal friends. We have seen superintendents who thought *they* were the job, that the district was *their* district. The terms "my staff" and "my district" are indicative of a false sense of pride and ownership. "Our" and "we" are terms denoting a broader, and realistic, perspective of what it takes to make a district work.

We do our very best for the district, but it always belongs to the people in the community, not us. The fact is that while we hold the title of superintendent, someone came before us, and someone will succeed us. A good reminder is from the front page of a newspaper with side-by-side articles the day after the untimely death of a city councilman. The article on the left described the circumstances of his death and the reaction of his family and colleagues. On the right was a story about two people the mayor was considering as replacements to fill the seat within the next few days. We do our jobs, but we are not our jobs.

However, we all get lost in our jobs, and no question about it, they are important. Education may be the most important—and rewarding—work in any society, and it is critical to democracy. But sometimes we lose our perspective about our jobs and ourselves. So we offer a few thoughts here that we have learned either the hard way through experience or from our trusted colleagues.

Always Think First

Board meetings present many issues and opportunities for discussion, disagreement, and action. Superintendents must be nimble and "quick on their decision-making feet" to deal with direct challenges, accusations, and gossip that beg for a response. But as Mark Twain advised, "It's better to be thought a fool than to open your mouth and prove it." We all know of superintendents, including ourselves, who wish they had not taken the bait by responding to a comment or question at a board meeting. It reminds us of a sign we saw under a mounted fish hanging over a fireplace: "If I had kept my mouth shut, I wouldn't be here now."

Superintendents who really know and believe in their personal values and the district's mission give a thoughtful response when a challenge is related to those beliefs. These leaders are also good at buying time in order to study an issue, and only then do they make an enlightened response. In this way, they correctly keep the focus on the issues, not the behavior of individuals.

Toughen Up—Hits Are Inevitable

Leadership isn't easy. Board agendas often contain difficult and controversial items such as boundary changes, staff reductions or dismissals, contentious litigation, discipline of students, choice of curriculum, or condemnation of land. The reality is almost always that these items are subjects of controversy.

The other reality is that people will sometimes attend and participate in board meetings who are angry, disrespectful, unprofessional, and downright unpleasant. When this happens, keep your focus on the issues and on the positive parts of the agenda, those where people are honored, awards are given, and the board discusses stimulating topics related to student achievement.

The hits, unfortunately, come with the territory. Even when angry people make comments that sound like personal attacks, for the most part they are upset at the issue and you represent a view different from theirs. As difficult as it is, try to see every negative situation as an opportunity to make something better.

Win With Dignity, Lose With Grace

Board meetings are not a sanctioned competitive sport. It is not a matter of earning points for our side, and there are no trophies for the victor.

However, most superintendents have competed for positions, taken university examinations, and enjoyed to some degree the power of the position. An unfortunate cliché is that a good superintendent is one who knows how to count to three, or five, whatever the majority number of trustees on the board. The tendency to want things to go our way is natural, especially when we have worked hard to prepare an item for board action and know our recommendation rests on firm ground.

When the board approves our recommendation, we acknowledge the fine work by the staff that led to this outcome. Conversely, we must accept that at times our recommendations will not be approved. This can be due to timing, special circumstances, and/or political conditions. If you have made several attempts to move the board, but a majority continues to advocate a different position, you may need to stop pushing. At those moments, we must decide how far to push and whether the issue is worth reconsidering, restructuring, or modifying or if we simply accept the decision and move on. When you let go, remember to do it with dignity. Accepting loss with dignity means carrying out the board's decision without expressing your disagreement. The difference of opinion is over, so you move on calmly and with respect for the responsibility of the board to make decisions.

"Open Door" and "Doormat" Are Not Synonyms

Leadership students are taught the value of having an open door. It is a good thing. It demonstrates your openness and enhances staff morale. While this is true, having an open door must be balanced so all your time is not swallowed up and you are detracted from completing your work.

Closing your door is perfectly acceptable. Your assistant can tell people you are busy on a project, and they are welcome to make an appointment. If you are generally visible and available, and frequently seen in the schools and community, people will understand. A concern is created only when the superintendent is always behind closed doors or always out of the office.

One superintendent's office is divided into two spaces, one for meeting with the public and one for quiet reflective work. With the skillful help of the administrative assistant, the superintendent has a private space for reading, working on the computer, and holding quiet conversations. A demanding visitor is directed to the public office where there are coffee and snacks, and the desk is uncluttered, organized, and inviting. The openness of the office and the willingness of the superintendent to meet do not detract from completing work until he can meet with the guest.

You Serve the Public, But Are Not a Servant

Many superintendents have heard people, especially angry ones, say, "I pay your salary with my taxes." To some degree that is correct and you could probably send the speaker a check for the portion of your salary his taxes pay. Nonetheless, your integrity, emotions, and values are not for sale. Working for the public does not give the public the right to be rude and disrespectful toward you.

The reality is, the superintendent works in a public and open environment. The issues coming to your office are focused on people's children, effective use of resources, and educational change. Of course, as superintendent you must use your best professional language in these volatile situations. You are the symbolic leader for the educational community. As one superintendent told us, "I was hired to make things better, not to become the problem." Yet there are times, hopefully rare, when a superintendent must describe for others what proper demeanor and decorum are.

Take Care of Your Health

We recommend taking time to read *The Power of Full Engagement*. Authors Jim Loehr and Tony Schwartz discuss the stressors in modern life and promote personal resilience. Their argument that our productivity depends on the quality of our physical, emotional, intellectual, and spiritual energy is quite persuasive. All of these areas are vital to overall health.

For superintendents who think they are indispensable, the amazing fact is that if they could not come to work, the district would not shut down, but continue on. Remember the city councilman? If the superintendent cannot leave others in charge, the question is, what leadership capacity is that superintendent building? Everyone needs time away to gain perspective. And that includes the staff—who probably could use some time without you.

Sadly, we know many superintendents who rarely take a vacation. We think this is a mistake. Smart boards insist that superintendents take their full vacation time. One highly successful superintendent we know insisted that every high-level administrator take three consecutive weeks off each year. Guess what? The district not only survived, it prospered. Another superintendent new to a district said in his address to the management team at their back-to-school retreat that he always took all of his vacation and he expected them to do the same. He received an ovation and the gratitude of people who worked very hard every day and wanted the time away to renew and refresh with their families.

We suggest you put "exercise" on specific days and times on your calendars, just as you calendar meetings. One tool for focusing on your health is the Covey and Associates planning calendar (see www.franklincovey .com for ordering information) that allows a space for "sharpening the saw," which requires setting aside time for physical and intellectual exercise. This is a difficult area for superintendents since it is possible to work continuously and not take time for personal health and exercise activities. In fact, they may be praised for their tireless work ethic, but actuarial tables remind us that such praise is hollow when stress and poor habits take their toll. In addition, we recommend that superintendent employment contracts require annual physicals. Once again, we say, you are truly the only person who can take care of your health.

Laugh—Bring Joy

> Albert Schweitzer employed humor as a form of . . . therapy. . . . His use of humor, in fact, was so artistic that one had the feeling he almost regarded it as a musical instrument. Some people, in the grip of uncontrollable laughter, say their ribs are hurting. The expression is probably accurate, but it is a delightful "hurt" that leaves the individual relaxed almost to the point of an open sprawl. It is the kind of "pain," too, that most people would do well to experience every day of their lives.
>
> (*Anatomy of an Illness,* Norman Cousins, 1980, p. 82)

Read the research—laughter is good for you. It helped Cousins fight cancer. There are many other stories about people who used laughter's mystical power to heal and bring perspective. We are talking about using techniques such as laughing at ourselves, silly movies and stories, and knee-slapping anecdotes. It is having simple, plain, good fun with family, friends, and colleagues. Laughter should uplift, and it should never be at the expense of others. Sarcasm may be clever, but it hurts someone and only increases the stress and alienation.

Leadership retreats ought to have fun built in as part of the agenda. The wonderful conductor Ben Zander tells us about Rule #6, "Don't take yourself so seriously!" (Labarre, 1998, p. 110). What are the other rules? There aren't any!

This view is echoed in *Lighten Up!,* a book that grew out of the authors' work with children with terminal illnesses. What they learned from children are lessons for those of us who forget the line between being serious about our work, but not ourselves. They identified an odd, yet prevalent disease—TP, which stands for Terminal Professionalism. Fortunately, there is a program to combat TP. Humaerobics is an Outward Bound training program for the terminally serious; it provides hope for those with a flabby sense of humor (Metcalf, 1992)!

To us, schools and entire school districts should be places of joy. What is more exciting than learning, opening new frontiers, and sharing the wisdom of the ages? There are so many ways to bring joy to your work and to yourself. Think of the great stories that happen every day in a school district. Just recalling them makes you feel better. We have a favorite cartoon that shows bent-over, grumpy adults going in one door of an Adult Rehab Center and coming out the other smiling and turning cartwheels. When you share the joys of education, you lift up everyone around you—and yourself! Share your sense of fun with others. Make part of your job adult rehab!

For Whom You Work Is Your Decision

As the district leader, there may be a night when you arrive home from a tough board meeting and the recovery techniques fail to create the desired wellness. Even with good health, a supportive friend or spouse, or other never-fail relief, there is a gnawing sense that things are not right. While it may be understandable that this discomfort happens occasionally, if it persists over time, it may be time to update the resume. No job is worth your life; no job is worth sacrificing your integrity.

Protect Your Integrity

The best recovery method is to be at home following the meeting, content knowing that regardless of the outcome of the decisions, you made the recommendations based on what is right for students, employees, the board, and the community. We were hired to do things right, but the best stress reducer is our knowing we did the right things. The legacy left by a superintendent might be due to balanced budgets, skillful negotiations, or efficient operations. However, it is more likely that a meaningful legacy will be based on the building of personal relationships, dedication to a vision, and open communication.

Keeping perspective about the importance of the role of the superintendent can help us recover from challenging times. We recently observed a successful superintendent addressing a class of future administrators, and we were impressed with his answer to a query from an aspiring superintendent. The questioner asked, "We have been to board meetings and we read the papers and see the headlines about all of the stressful incidents that happen. Why should we put ourselves in that position?"

The experienced superintendent replied that it was the unexpected challenges, the perplexing interactions, the complexity of problems that made the job a wonderful opportunity for leadership. Comparing his opportunities of leading a school district to his military service, he told the listeners that both entailed conflict and difficult decisions. Both professions are vitally important to a democracy. He said passionately that meeting with a board in a democracy to do significant work for children was an honor. We think he is right, and honor is the perfect word for the opportunity we have been given.

11

Wrapping Up

You'd better wave back to the guy in the pickup, because he may be on your board after the next election.

(Colleague superintendent)

We'll admit it. No matter how much you and your staff have done to ensure the board meeting will be effective, unexpected things will happen. In a very real way, that's what often contributes to the stress that both superintendents and board members experience prior to and during the meetings. As we have emphasized, the major point is that board meetings that improve student achievement, model good teaching and learning, and respect the governance role of the board and the executive responsibilities of the superintendent do not happen by accident. They require conscious attention and effort through a set of specific strategies and actions we have discussed throughout this book.

Having said that, let's turn to another dimension of board meetings that deserves our final attention—the political, social, and economic context in which board meetings occur. Peter Drucker's comments in *Managing the Non-Profit Agency* offer perspective for this context.

When you look at the school board . . . you have a multiplicity of constituencies—each of which can say no and none of which can say yes. The multiplicity of constituencies is reflected in your

board, your trustees, who are likely to be intensely involved in
running the agency. You could say public schools are governmental,
but the school board is not governmental. It has the constituency
role. That's what causes all the difficulty for superintendents. They
are really public service agencies rather than government agencies.
(Drucker, 1992, p. 17)

The best planning practices, the best guidelines for the orderly conduct
of board meetings, and the best guidelines for post-meeting follow-up significantly diminish the likelihood of problems. However, the political context in which board members individually and boards collectively operate
leaves the door open to those behaviors and events that cause most superintendents to enter every board meeting with two fingers crossed behind
their backs. Drucker's comments remind us that as elected officials, board
members have obligations to constituencies. Developing an understanding of how these obligations are created and how they may guide individual behaviors is important for every superintendent. In fact, the conduct of
board members at the meeting is often determined by the relationships
between board members and their constituents.

At any given board meeting, political issues may surface. As elected
officials, board members have spent money and campaigned to win. Many
have made campaign promises; they will be reminded of these promises
by the community groups or individuals who come to meetings for that
very purpose. In some cases, these groups include representatives from
employee groups who have put money into board member campaigns.
The "public communications" period is when these individuals and
groups are most likely to surface. This is the time when the fingers behind
the back cross even tighter.

Political issues are often present even before a new superintendent
starts his or her job. In one urban district, the position became open after
the dismissal of a superintendent following two years of contentious
issues involving board–superintendent relations, the unions, and the
press. The politics began with a public search conducted by a firm that
charged $125,000. The public interviewed four finalists who all dropped
out due to the publicity concerning the interview or pressure to stay
in their current roles. The press was critical of the search, and employees claimed the money should have been spent on classroom needs.
Frustrated, the board conducted a second search at a cost of $85,000. This
one was confidential. A candidate was successfully recruited and selected
but began his work in the midst of a controversy for which he was not
responsible.

If the internal politics are not complicated enough, a new trend adds
more challenges to the public meeting. It is not uncommon for city mayors
to seek control over the governance of local schools. New York, Chicago,
and smaller cities frequently make news as mayors decry the condition of

public schools and seek power to appoint board members, superintendents, and even make curricular decisions. One mayor of a large city recently told the press that the local school district was "committing socioeconomic murder of children." His answer to raising the test scores of disadvantaged children was to allow him to appoint the school board and select the superintendent. In this case, the mayor appointed two full-time education advisors to his staff to monitor the actions of the local board. More strikingly, he added these positions during a time of financial stress and other personnel reductions in the city. The potential for stressful relationships between elected school board members and strong mayors with the superintendent in the middle is obvious.

The political context is further complicated by the increased role of state and federal governments in the funding and management of schools. Government sets the rules and then provides the money only when it is attached to certain conditions, most of which are identified as a result of a very political process. Add to this the fact that most states have governors who campaigned on some type of educational improvement agenda. But ignoring the governors or even legislators for that matter creates its own inherent risk.

Perhaps a local columnist covering the education scene in one city said it best: "In the current environment, there will never be a superintendent who can stay above the politics stirred by the district's critics. This is a school system that loves to hate its leaders" (Davis, 2003). Negative behavior heightens the responsibility of the superintendent to model good teaching and learning by creating a leadership plan for the board meetings that keeps the focus on student achievement.

Just as political issues impact board meetings, so do social and economic ones. Rapid changes in demographics, downturns in the economy, tensions between ethnic groups, crime rates, and more are the context in which boards have to meet their responsibilities to educate each child in the community. Two school districts in central California serve as excellent case studies to document the challenges and opportunities of changing demographics and socioeconomic realities. The ethnic diversity of the two communities is 85% other than white with over 90% of the students qualifying for free federal lunch programs. Both communities asked citizens and employees to list the qualities and characteristics they desired for their next superintendent.

Communication skills and high expectations for student achievement were first on both lists. People wanted a leader who would bring a sincere appreciation for diversity and cultural awareness, but not excuses for low achievement or a patronizing attitude toward members of ethnically diverse populations. Constituents of those districts took "No Child Left Behind" literally, although some members of the political elite worried that caring for all children might challenge the status quo that gave privilege to a few.

At first glance, these larger political, social, and economic issues may seem to have little to do with teaching and learning. A closer look reveals otherwise. While these issues may suggest that accomplishing the mission-critical work of the district will not be easy, they also present the superintendent with an opportunity to use this context as a means of *advancing* the mission-critical work.

We offer seven ways superintendents can use the context to advance the district's mission. First is for the superintendents to keep their own communication at the board meeting effective and focused. Superintendents must understand the economy of language. Simply stated, at the board meeting we must listen more, say less, and talk about what matters most. In the political world of public meetings, the "toothpaste theory" applies: You can squeeze it out, but you can never get it back in the tube.

One superintendent, in attempting to explain multicultural issues to the board, used a controversial ethnic term. It took many months to recover. Another superintendent learned the hard way that with the press nothing is ever "off the record" when the criticism he made of one of his board members was in the paper the next day. Today's successful superintendents practice what they are going to say with trusted advisors prior to making public statements. They use coaches if possible and recognize that "shooting from the hip" is analogous to a career death wish.

Our second suggestion is to take time to think and reflect during periods of pressure. One superintendent reported on working with a coach who advised using an authentic communication model when giving controversial news at the meeting. The model begins with some version of the statement, "The harsh reality is. . . ." This is followed by, "My part in it is. . . ." The model concludes with, "And what I need from you is. . . ." For example, "The harsh reality is that I must recommend budget cuts to the board and the community due to the funding situation. My part in this situation is to communicate the budget clearly to the board, the staff, the media, and those affected. What I need from you, as board members, is for you to expect accurate information on a regular basis." This is not a panacea formula, but is one way to structure ideas and concepts for a board meeting in a stressful political time.

A third way is to demonstrate sincere and timely interest in the community where you serve and lead. The superintendent must not appear as an outsider who lacks an understanding of the culture and dynamics of the community. One superintendent inherited a yearly retreat for administrators to plan for the coming year held in a comfortable, resort-type setting where the leadership team talked about the plight of the disadvantaged children and the achievement gap. The next year, the superintendent changed the concept by adopting the theme "Grow Where You're Planted" and sending the administrators to meet with community agencies, ethnic leaders, political leaders, and neighborhood associations, who joined the retreat. Keynote speakers included parents representing ethnic groups in the district who described what they wanted for their children.

At the subsequent board meeting, participants reported they were more invigorated, inspired, and ready to begin work than they were under the previous format. Many senior leaders agreed that they now better understood the needs of neighborhood schools. Others reported they had forged new relationships with elected officials, media leaders, and spokespersons for ethnic groups. Board comments expressed pleasure at the responsiveness to and by the community. The back-to-school headlines were quite a change from the previous year's, which had criticized the superintendent for spending dollars to host a fancy retreat. This type of new, politically savvy leadership is necessary for today's superintendents in these political times.

A fourth way is to have policies in place to regulate the handling of technical matters such as roll call votes, when a super majority vote is required, and election of officers. We choose simple over complex and recommend that boards seriously consider whether it is always necessary to observe Robert's Rules. Those rules were designed to guide the conduct of large governing bodies such as legislatures and parliaments and may be overly complex for smaller groups. One simple way to operate is this: The ruling of the board president stands unless it is challenged by a board member. In that case, a majority vote could overturn. A compromise would be to operate by a simple set of rules and use Robert's Rules only as a backup.

Fifth is to avoid scheduling a vote on most major items (except those of an emergency nature) until input from key stakeholders has been received and the board has had the opportunity to deliberate and consider each board member's viewpoint and the superintendent's recommendation.

A sixth way is to remember the direct link between the board meeting and student achievement. What the district wants to occur in every classroom and every school should be modeled at the board meeting. It is as simple as agreeing never to embarrass or degrade anyone in public; respectful behavior is what we want staff and students to use with each other. Or it is as difficult as deciding how to vote on a new graduation requirement or school closure. Remember that people are closely watching you and the board and how you operate. Behaviors that are inconsistent with what is being requested of teachers and students are quickly recognized. Media coverage that accompanies board meetings leaves the public impression, for better or worse, that "that's how we do things around here."

Our last suggestion is to have in place a series of protocols to guide preparation, conduct, and follow-up from board meetings. Meeting protocols are helpful for any nonprofit board or for that matter any governing agency where political, social, and economic issues form a context that constantly threatens the proper exercise by the board of its governance role. For school boards, they are a necessity. Why? We are back to the idea of mission-critical work. As we have often said, our mission is teaching and learning. We know pressures will always exist, taking us away from that mission. Board policies concerned with voting processes, election of officers, and other parliamentary procedures are necessary, but insufficient.

What is needed is a specific set of protocols dealing with the board meeting conduct that reflects the practices suggested in this book and reflects your good sense about the board with whom you work and your school district and community. When developed collaboratively by the superintendent and board, these protocols become a reality check against which the superintendent and board may evaluate the extent to which they are accomplishing the mission-critical work of the district. And isn't that why all of us are here in the first place? We never want to lose the passion for high-quality teaching and learning, even in the midst of the inevitable challenging circumstances that come our way. The board meeting is a unique opportunity to instill the passion for teaching and learning in others; it is an opportunity we never want to miss.

Resource A

Board–Superintendent Protocols (Sample)

Note: This *sample* set of protocols focuses on leadership, governance, and management, as opposed to the board meeting itself. We recommend the board–superintendent team work together to develop a set of protocols such as these and put them in place before developing, again together, the actual board meeting protocols. This is a sample only. State school board associations have samples, as do many school districts across the nation, and many can be accessed via district Web sites.

Purpose: The board of trustees is the educational policymaking body for the district. To effectively meet the district's challenges, the board and superintendent must function together as a leadership team. To ensure unity among team members, effective protocols—operating procedures—must be in place. There are general protocols for the board and superintendent, protocols specifically for the board, and protocols specifically for the superintendent.

AS MEMBERS OF THE BOARD AND AS SUPERINTENDENT, WE WILL . . .

1. Keep teaching and learning as the primary focus of our work.

2. Value, respect, and support public education.

3. Model good learning by participating in professional development.

4. Respect the differences between governance and management.

5. Recognize and respect differences of perspective and style on the board and among staff, students, parents, and the community.

6. Operate with trust and integrity.

7. Keep confidential matters confidential.

AS A BOARD, WE WILL . . .

1. Understand that the authority of the board rests with the board as a whole, and not individual board members.

2. Define the district's core values and beliefs.

3. Develop with the superintendent a vision of a district with high-performing students and staff.

4. Establish clear expectations for student success that promote equity of outcomes for all students.

5. Establish a structure that moves the district toward achievement of the vision, mission, core values, and strategic goals. This structure is established through the board's policymaking and policy-review function.

6. Make sure our agenda and behaviors reflect the district's core values and beliefs.

7. Govern in a dignified and professional manner, treating everyone with civility and respect.

8. Take collective responsibility for the board's performance.

9. Evaluate on a regular basis the board's effectiveness against a predetermined set of criteria.

10. Ensure there are opportunities for the diverse range of opinions and beliefs in the community to inform the board.

11. Involve the community, parents, students, and staff in developing a shared vision of district success that focuses on the progress of all students and staff toward meeting high standards.

12. Adopt, evaluate, and update policies that enable the district to achieve its vision, mission, core values, and strategic goals.

13. Adopt a budget that supports achievement of vision and mission, and monitor on a regular basis the fiscal health of the district.

14. Establish a framework for collective bargaining that supports high-quality teaching and learning.

15. Ensure that the district operates within the legal parameters established by local, state, and federal governmental agencies.

TO BUILD A STRONG SUPERINTENDENT–BOARD LEADERSHIP TEAM, THE BOARD WILL . . .

1. Hire and support a superintendent who will achieve the district's vision, mission, values, and goals.

2. Establish with the superintendent strategic goals that anticipate changes in the internal and external environment and reflect a commitment to continuous improvement.

3. Conduct regular and timely evaluations of the superintendent based on agreed-upon goals, established board directions, and district performance.

4. Commit time to building a team approach to governance based on open, honest communication.

AS SUPERINTENDENT, I WILL . . .

1. Work toward creating a team with the board that is dedicated to students.

2. Respect and acknowledge the board's role in setting policy and over-seeing the performance of the superintendent.

3. Work with the board to establish a clear vision for the school district.

4. Communicate the common vision.

5. Recognize that the board–superintendent governance relationship requires support from the district's management team.

6. Understand the distinction between board and staff roles, and respect the role of the board as the representative of the community.

7. Accept leadership responsibility and be accountable for implementing the vision, goals, and policies of the district.

8. Provide data to the board so it can make data-driven decisions.

9. Communicate with board members promptly and effectively.

10. Distribute information fully and equally to all board members.

11. Never bring a matter to a public meeting that is a surprise to the board.

12. Provide requests for additional information through a board update, special report, board agenda item, or as a board workshop or special meeting.

13. Represent the school district by being visible in the community.

14. Model the value of life-long learning.

15. Be the instructional leader of the district.

Resource B

Twelve–Month Calendar (Sample)

	July	August	September	October	November	Remaining months
Main Items	1. MOU-School Resource Officer 2. Disclosure report 3. SDCOE Outdoor Ed. Prog.	1. Accreditation 2. BTSA 3. ELL apps 4. 9th grade CSR	1. Grade Policy 2. Districtwide STAR results 3. FY Finance 4. VUTA Initial proposals 5. Goals Strategies	1. Update on growth mgmnt 2. Decision-CHSM 3. Quarterly investment report 4. Site reports: CHS, AOMS, VMS	1. CSR application 2. Boundary discussion for CMHS 3. Teachers teaching outside credentials	
Awards and Recognition			1. Classified employee of month	1. Classified employee of month	1. Classified employee of month 2. Recog. of Bd. Pres.	
Closed Session	1. Annual eval of Sup't	1. Eval and contract of Sup't	1. Property negotiations 2. VUTA negotiations 3. VUSE negotiations	1. Property negotiations 2. VUTA negotiations 3. VUSE negotiations	1. Property negotiations 2. VUTA negotiations 3. VUSE negotiations	
Special Meetings	1. Eval of Sup't 2. Comm. Vision-Setting workshop		1. Board governance workshop			

151

Resource C

Board Agenda Development Worksheet (Sample)

INDEPENDENT SCHOOL DISTRICT

BOARD AGENDA DEVELOPMENT WORKSHEET
For Board Meeting of January 12, 2005

A. AWARDS AND RECOGNITION
  1. Classified Employee of the Month

B. CONSENT CALENDAR
  1. General Administration
      a. Setting of Organizational
         Meeting
      b. Orchestra Trip to New York

  2. Curriculum and Instruction
      a. 2005–06 Class policy size
         (2nd reading)

  3. Business Services
      a. New and Replacement
         Equipment
      b. Service Contracts
      c. Disposal of Surplus Property
         Delivery Trucks
      d. Purchase Orders

  4. Personnel Services
      a. Personnel Action Report—
         Classified
      b. Personnel Action Report—
         Certificate
      c. Student Teacher Agreement

C. ACTION ITEMS
  1. General Administration
      a.

  2. Business Services
      a. Public hearing: 1st
         reading/action Ordinance
         #1–678 Auth levy of special
         taxes
      b. Donations

  3. Curriculum and Instruction
      a. AP Physics Curriculum
      b. English Lang. Learners
         Benchmarks

  4. Personnel Services

D. DISCUSSION/
    INFORMATION ITEMS
  1. General Administration
      a.

  2. Business Services
      a. Review District Budget

  3. Curriculum and Instruction
      a. 2003–04 Site Reports:
         Pine and Oak
      b. 1st Reading-rev.
         to BP-145-Grad Req.

  4. Personnel Services
      a.

CLOSED SESSION: Please provide exact wording for open and closed session agendas

  1. Student Expulsions

  2. Conference With a Real Property Negotiator

  3. Conference With Legal Counsel re: Anticipated Litigation

Resource D

Individual Agenda Item (Sample)

INDEPENDENT SCHOOL DISTRICT

Address

Office of Superintendent

BOARD MEETING AGENDA ITEM

To: Board of Education   Meeting Date:

From: Agenda Item:

Core Value:

Strategic Priority:

Subject:

Background Information:

Fiscal Impact:

Superintendent's Recommendation (in the form of a motion):

DISPOSITION BY BOARD OF EDUCATION

Motion by: _____   Seconded by: _____

Approved: _____ Not Approved: _____ Tabled: _____

Resource E

Welcome to the Board Meeting (Sample)

WELCOME TO THE
INDEPENDENT SCHOOL DISTRICT
MEETING OF THE BOARD OF EDUCATION

Your Board of Trustees welcomes you to its meetings and encourages your constructive participation. This welcome letter has been prepared to review some of the procedures followed by the Board of Trustees in conducting necessary district business and to advise you on how to participate in the process. In order for the board to do its job thoughtfully and efficiently, your cooperation is requested in observing the following procedures.

Sources of Board Authority

1. The Constitution of the state
2. The State Education Code as adopted by the State Legislature
3. Policies and procedures of this Board

What to do if you wish to address the board

If the item is on the agenda:

If you wish to speak before the board, we would appreciate your filling out the attached card and indicating the agenda item number. Please hand the card to the secretary prior to the meeting. When the subject is under consideration, you will be called upon by the Board President to make your comments.

If the item is not on the agenda:

We would appreciate your completing the attached card and handing it to the secretary prior to the start of the meeting. You will be called upon and allowed 3 minutes to make your presentation; however, according to law, the board cannot take action on items not on the agenda.

Personal comments:

Complaints against employees will normally be heard in closed session, and the District's complaint procedure should be followed.

Normally an attempt should be made to resolve problems or make requests through the appropriate staff of the District prior to addressing the Governing Board.

Resource F

Request to Speak Cards (Samples)

**Board of Education
Unified School District**

Agenda Item: _____ Date: _____

Subject: _____

_____

Name: _____

Occupation: _____

Address: _____

Telephone: _____

**Request to Speak
Independent School District
Board of Trustees Meeting**

If you wish to address the board,
please complete and give to the secretary.

Maximum speaking time: 3 minutes are permitted.

Name: _____

Date: _____

Address: _____

City: _____ ZIP: _____ Phone: _____

Representing: Self: _____ Organization: _____

Topic/Question: _____

_____

_____

References

Abrashoff, D. M. (2002). *It's your ship.* New York: Warner.

Baldwin, J. (1961). *Nobody knows my name: More notes of a native son.* New York: Dial Press.

Boren, J. (2004, April 11). [Editorial]. *The Fresno Bee,* p. B10.

Carlzon, J. (1987). *Moments of truth.* New York: Ballinger.

Carver, J. (1997). *Boards that make a difference: A new design for leadership in nonprofit and public organizations.* San Francisco: Jossey-Bass.

Cohen, B., & Greenfield, J. (1997). *Ben & Jerry's double-dip.* New York: Fireside.

Covey, S. (1990). *Seven habits of highly effective people.* New York: Fireside.

Cousins, N. (1980). *Anatomy of an illness as perceived by the patient.* Boston: G. K. Hall.

Cvsa, V., Jansen, P., & Kilpatrick, A. (2003). *The dynamic board: Lessons from high-performing nonprofits.* Washington, DC: McKinsey.

Davis, J. (2003, December 13). Fresno County's top educator blasted. *The Fresno Bee,* p. A1.

Drucker, P. (1992). *Managing the non-profit organization: Practice and principles.* New York: HarperBusiness.

DuFour, R. (2001, Winter). In the right context. *Journal of Staff Development, 22, 1.* Oxford, OH: National Staff Development Council.

Frankl, V. (1984). *Man's search for meaning.* New York: Simon & Schuster.

Goodman, R. H., Fulbright, L., & Zimmerman, W. G., Jr. (1997). *Getting there from here.* Boston: Educational Research Service.

Johnston, G. L., Gross, G. E., Townsend, R. S., Lynch, P., Novotney, P. B., Roberts, B., Garcy, L., & Gil, L. (2002). *Eight at the top: A view inside public education.* Lanham, MD: Scarecrow Press.

King, G. (Director). (1949). *Twelve o' clock high* [motion picture]. United States: Twentieth Century Fox.

Labarre, P. (1998, December). Leadership—Ben Zander. *Fast Company, 20,* p. 110.

Langewiesche, W. (1998, March). The lessons of ValuJet 592. *Atlantic Monthly,* pp. 82–98.

Loehr, J., & Schwartz, T. (2003). *The power of full engagement.* New York: Free Press.

Lundin, S. (Writer) (1998). *Fish!* [video]. Produced by ChartHouse, International Learning Corporation, Burnsville, MN.

Mandela, N. (1994). *Long road to freedom.* Boston: Little, Brown.

Melville, H. (2002). *Moby Dick.* New York: W.W. Norton.

Milne, A. A. (1926). *Winnie-the-Pooh.* New York: Dutton.

Metcalf, C. W., & Felible, R. (1992). *Lighten up.* Boston: Addison-Wesley.

Nair, K. (1994). *A higher standard of leadership: Lessons from the life of Gandhi.* San Francisco: Berrett-Koehler.

Peters, T. (1982). *In search of excellence.* New York: Warner.

Pritchett, P., & Muirhead, B. (1998). *The Mars pathfinder.* Dallas: Pritchett.

Speigel, S. (Producer), Lean, D. (Director), & Boulle, P. (Screenplay). (1983). *Bridge on the River Kwai* [motion picture]. Great Britain: Horizon Pictures; United States: Columbia Pictures.

Tichy, N. (1997). *The leadership engine: How winning companies build leaders at every level.* New York: HarperBusiness.

Wooden, J. (1997). *They call me coach.* New York: McGraw-Hill.

Index

**CORWIN
PRESS**

The Corwin Press logo—a raven striding across an open book—represents the union of courage and learning. Corwin Press is committed to improving education for all learners by publishing books and other professional development resources for those serving the field of K–12 education. By providing practical, hands-on materials, Corwin Press continues to carry out the promise of its motto: **"Helping Educators Do Their Work Better."**